"This book is a masterpiece! I am going to make it required reading for everyone who works in my agency!"

—Eric Yaverbaum, best-selling author
Manager Partner of LIME
public relations and promotion

"If you're easily tongue-tied or a verbal klutz, Ilise Benun's guide to asserting yourself at work helps with dozens of confidence-building tools. You'll especially appreciate the suggestions for what to say in specific situations."

—Marcia Yudkin, author
6 Steps to Free Publicity

"Ilise Benun's excellent new book is about shy people, but it's for everyone. If you're shy, Ilise Benun will help you have the maximum opportunity to be successful—and it won't hurt. If you're an employer, there's a good change you have some shy employees. Helping them is not only good business, it's the right thing to do. If you love a shy person, you've just found the next present you're going to give them."

—Jim Blasingame, author
Three Minutes to Success,
and award-winning host of the
Small Business Advocate Show

"They say the world can be divided into extroverts and introverts. What Benun understands and conveys in both word and tone is that when it comes to effectively managing situations where our own ego is at risk, we could all use some help. Most importantly, in this wonderfully warm yet powerful guide, she provides real-world solutions we all can use effectively. She doesn't just identify the issues, she shows us what we can do about them."

—Dave Opton, founder & CEO
of ExecuNet, the original
executive career management
and recruiting network

"Ilise Benun shows individuals how to recognize their value and be willing to stand up for it—and claim the rewards and satisfaction that comes from being listened to and respected. Generations have grown up being told 'don't brag' and 'go along with things.' Relatively few have been told to respect—and fight for—their right to be heard. Our parents tell us to be compliant and "behave," but bosses and clients reward those who can, non-abrasively, speak up and speak out. I can name 20 people who should get this book. More important, if I had this book 10 or 20 years ago, I would be happily retired and living on top of a Montana mountain or along the California coast!"

—Roger C. Parker, author
Streetwise Relationship Marketing on the Internet and the best-selling
Looking Good in Print

STOP PUSHING ME AROUND!

STOP PUSHING ME AROUND!

A Workplace Guide
for the Timid, Shy, and Less Assertive

by Ilise Benun

CAREER PRESS

The Career Press, Inc.
Franklin Lakes, NJ

STOP PUSHING ME AROUND!
EDITED AND TYPESET BY ASTRID DERIDDER
Cover design by Rob Johnson/Johnson Design
Printed in the U.S.A. by Book-mart Press

To order this title, please call toll-free 1-800-CAREER-1 (NJ and Canada: 201-848-0310) to order using VISA or MasterCard, or for further information on books from Career Press.

B CAREER
PRESS

The Career Press, Inc., 3 Tice Road, PO Box 687,
Franklin Lakes, NJ 07417
www.careerpress.com

Library of Congress Cataloging-in-Publication Data

Benun, Ilise, 1961-
    Stop pushing me around! : a workplace guide for the timid, shy, and less assertive / by Ilise Benun.
        p. cm.
    Includes index.
    ISBN-13: 978-1-56414-882-7
    ISBN-10: 1-56414-882-3 (paper)
        1. Psychology, Industrial. 2. Assertiveness (Psychology) 3. Interpersonal relations. 4. Business communication. I. Title.

HF5548.8.B378 2006
650.1'3--dc22

                                            2006043908

Acknowledgments

This book is the first physical evidence of a process that started long ago. I have been marinating these ideas for the past 20 years, well before I was even aware of it. None of them are mine—I can only take credit for arranging them in this order.

I've tried to write a book about speaking up and reaching out, and in the process I have learned a lot. I have spoken up (sometimes forcing myself) and reached out to people around the world. I can barely keep track (so forgive any omissions) of all the friends, clients, and colleagues I relied on for feedback, and who generously took their time to work with me on these ideas: Alan Seiden, Doug Dolan, Colleen Cannon, Belinda Plutz, David Tornabene, Neil Tortorella, Beth Harrison, Alina Lee, Sheila Campbell, Jose Angel Santana, Lea Ann Hutter, Lauri Baram, Ivan Drucker, Patrick Malloy, Mario Sen and Tiffany, Kathleen Ogle, Donna Olah-Reiken, Mark Gerstmann, Stuart Cowan, and Carol Dilley. Many thanks also to Carol Dilley and John Casey. Many thanks to Jim Blasingame of the Small Business Advocate, who contributed ideas during our early morning radio conversations.

Those who were patient and helpful through the writing process include Marilyn Matos, Kathleen Harrington (and little Sammy, born just as I was finishing the writing), Susan Taylor, Khephra Burns, Linda Rothschild, Edward Hindin, Peleg Top, and Eric Yaverbaum.

I would also like to thank my clients, whose lives I learn from every day: Bob Bly, Debra Hamilton, Karen Zapp and John Withers, Mistina Bates, Carol Nadell, Kurt Krause, Janey Saavedra, Lloyd Dangle, Scott Souchock, Stephanie Aaron, Joan Damico, Peter Levinson, Louis Beauregard, Joanne Sullivan, Don Forschmidt, Celia Siegel, and Maryan Binkley.

I am also grateful to everyone who contributed their ideas on my blog, those who passed along information, and those who found books or pointed to articles. And all the writers whose works I read as part of my research: Dr. Susan Lipkins, Dave Opton, and Lauryn Franzoni at ExecuNet; David Reynolds; Gregg and Linda Krech at the To Do Institute; Steve Krug; and many more.

Thanks especially to Roger C. Parker, who planted the seed of this idea in my mind when he heard the title of my workshop at the AWAI Bootcamp, *Interpersonal Skills for Introverts*, and said, "That needs to be a book."

Thanks also to all the folks at Career Press, for all their efforts to nurture that seed into this book, and especially my agent, Lynn Haller at Studio B, who played the role of shepherd.

And finally, this book wouldn't have been possible without the help of my teachers and colleagues at The Relationships Lab: Dr. Joseph Simo, Melodie Somers, Dennis Drew, John Lenzi, Amy Beer, Jeff Chancas, Loren Sherman, Ellen Coleman, Lisa Miller, Arthur Kilduff, Kim Knowlton, Caryn Browning, as well as my writing teachers, especially Philip Schultz and The Writer's Studio. Thank you all so much.

Contents

Section III: Communication Cheat Sheets

Introduction

Like all of us, I am a work in progress. I am not the shy one who got over my fears and wrote to tell about it. Unfortunately, that's just not what happened.

I am neither the wallflower nor the master networker. Although I was pretty quiet as a kid, I'm not a naturally shy person. And yet, as with everyone, I have my shy moments when I don't know what to say, or suddenly feel afraid to make a phone call. I enjoy talking to people but sometimes, when an acquaintance gets on the bus, I bury my head in a newspaper for reasons I can't always explain.

One recent experience has particularly influenced me regarding the idea that if I choose to do things that are uncomfortable, I will learn a lot from the experience. In my consulting practice I took on a client who scared me at first. Not because he was a monster or abusive in any way. There was just something about his manner, his language, and his way of interacting that "pushed my buttons." I was no longer the middle-aged professional having a meeting with a prospective client. Suddenly, I had traveled back in time to a place where I was a little girl facing a big scary person.

In my first meeting with this client, I came close to tears in response to something he said (or, more accurately, something I heard). If I had broken down, he would have been flabbergasted, because he had no idea what was going on. I didn't either, for that matter. When I left that meeting, I had a choice to make. I could continue to work with him (he needed my help, it was clear) or not. As I thought it through and discussed it with various friends and colleagues, I came up with all sorts of reasons not to continue. But the bottom line was: I was uncomfortable and I didn't like it. Yet I couldn't blame him for that feeling. Somewhere in the back of my mind, I knew this was a chance to do something different, to be someone different, to transform that little girl into a woman who could handle this guy and whatever happened while working with him.

I chose to go forward and I am so glad I did. Over the course of the project, I did the time travel more than once (and more often that I would have preferred.) But each time, I noticed—"Oh, I am defensive again"—and in the moment, tried to do something different. By the end of the project, I was catching the defensive comments before they escaped my mouth and offering a different response.

This client and I have done excellent work together, and there is potential for much more. He is intelligent, direct, and demanding, but he is also reasonable and has a great sense of humor. What I see most clearly now is that although I was looking directly at him, I wasn't seeing him at all that first day. My attention was focused inward, and all I saw was a man who sounded mean and was trying to push me around. We learned to joke about it—and now it doesn't even happen anymore.

—Ilise Benun

So You're Not a People Person

1

Getting to Know Yourself Better

Andy is an extremely intelligent computer programmer who considers himself shy. He likes his work but wishes he could be left alone to do it. He works in a small family-owned software development business run by an insecure boss. This boss promised Andy a bonus last year, but it hasn't been mentioned since. Andy would like to speak to his boss about the bonus, but he never knows when his boss will be in a good mood and he doesn't know how to approach it, so he hasn't said anything.

●●●

Kathy, a self-employed graphic designer, cringes at the thought of approaching "strangers" at networking functions. She is a wonderful designer and has been lucky, because most of her work has come by word of mouth. Kathy says she doesn't have the confidence to talk to strangers. She can't bring herself to attend a networking meeting, even though once she's there, she usually has a great time.

What does Andy mean when he says he's shy? What is the confidence Kathy needs to put on her coat and go to a gathering of strangers? Let's begin by defining our terms.

what is shyness?

Webster's defines shy as "easily frightened" and "disposed to avoid a person or thing." Bernardo Carducci, director of the Shyness Research Institute at Indiana University–Southeast, says that shy people are slow to warm up, have a limited comfort zone, and avoid approaching strangers.

what is confidence?

According to Webster's, confidence is "a feeling or consciousness of one's powers or of reliance on one's circumstances" and "faith or belief that one will act in a right, proper and effective way." In other words, to be confident is to know you can handle whatever comes along, which you probably can.

Andy is frightened to ask about his bonus and is avoiding the subject. And Kathy is afraid to approach a stranger because she doesn't think she'll be able to handle herself in an impromptu conversation.

Gregg Krech, a leading authority on Japanese psychology and the author of the book *Naikan: Gratitude, Grace and the Japanese Art of Self-Reflection* writes, "In the center of [a shy person's] anxious feeling is the seed of the desire to achieve, to transcend, to be worthy. The real problem is not these feelings in and of themselves; it is that we are letting this particular group of feelings 'push us around.'"

It may feel as though we are being pushed around by coworkers, bosses, and clients, but we're actually doing it to ourselves. The assertiveness we need to learn should not be addressed towards the pushy boss or coworkers; instead we need to learn to be assertive with ourselves and our feelings so we can achieve our goals. Even if you've been shy all your life and it feels natural, there are things you can do to expand your horizon and bring you out of your shell. Benefits—even riches—await those who can speak up and reach out.

who is shy?

Carducci, also the author of *Shyness: A Bold New Approach*, has been studying shyness since the early 1980s. He asserts that the number of Americans who consider themselves shy has hovered around 40 percent for the past 25 years. That's a lot of shy people! No matter how much it feels like you're the only one, you are not alone. The ranks of the shy include men and women, young and old, salaried and self-employed. They come from across the professional spectrum, from the top of the corporate ladder to the bottom, and can be found in all industries, from information technology and accounting to advertising, publishing, and the world of fashion design.

It's not always easy to believe that shyness is so widespread because many shy people don't appear to be shy. In other words, there are many seemingly outgoing people who feel shy or who see themselves as shy, but it's not always evident to the outside world. And there are many who masquerade as extroverts because they have to—CEOs, performers, and media-savvy people who spend lots of time in the limelight. Some of the more famous ones include Carol Burnett, Johnny Carson, Barbara Walters, and Al Gore.

In fact, we all have shy moments when facing a new challenge or an unknown person. The only difference is that some of us let it hold us back whereas others don't. That's a choice you can make.

shyness and biology: genes, temperament, and brains

For many people, shyness feels innate. But are people born shy? Is your temperament dictated by your genetics? According to a study reported in the *Wall Street Journal* in early 2006, scientists have discovered a "shy gene" called 5-HTT. However, not everyone born with this gene becomes a shy child or a shy adult. It only lives up to its name when you grow up in a certain type of environment.

In other words, if you have the shy gene and you were raised in an environment where your parents had little social support and you were protected from the world—instead of encouraged to venture out into it—you may have become a shy adult. However, if you have the shy gene but were raised in a strong community with many adults attentively teaching you what you needed to learn, and by parents who made a conscious and consistent effort to get you out to play with other kids despite your reluctance, you are more likely to have grown out of your shyness.

Researchers have also attributed shyness to natural temperament. There is evidence that approximately 15 to 20 percent of infants are born with what Dr. Jerome Kagan of Harvard University (Kagan, 1994) and his colleagues (Kagan, Reznick, & Snidman, 1988) refer to as an "inhibited temperament." Inhibited children are those who are easily aroused or excited. They are the ones who, at two years of age, might be more likely to hide behind a parent's legs when a stranger enters their play area. They are the ones who, at seven, play by themselves instead of with other children. Carducci proposes that this inhibited behavior begins to be labeled by parents, teachers, and acquaintances as shyness. Shy behaviors then become habits that are strengthened as we mature.

Luckily, the opposite may be true as well. "Parents who engineer gradual emboldening experiences to their shy children provide a lifelong corrective to the fearfulness," writes Daniel Goleman in his best-selling book, *Emotional Intelligence*. He also cites statistics that one in three infants born with an inhibited temperament lose their timidity by kindergarten.

●●●

Beyond our genes and our temperament, we have our brains, which also play a role in shyness. Here's how it works: When you learn a new skill, your brain actually changes. If you wanted to learn to use a computer, for example, your brain would arrange a new neural pathway for learning to use a computer. As you learn, this new pathway develops. The more you practice, the more proficient you become, and the more your brain changes, until your brain gradually develops the neural pathways to make your "practicing" become automatic. Soon, you don't have to focus and you can type and click and open documents without even thinking about it. You've learned to do something new. Experience sculpts the brain. Everything we learn changes our brain and becomes part of our neural pathways. We've known for awhile that a child's brain has a remarkable plasticity to change as a child learns and develops. More recent studies on the adult brain also demonstrate an astounding ability to create new neural pathways, even as we age. For example, memory-enhancing exercises and intellectual stimulation have been proven to keep the brain evolving.

Although you may not realize it, you have more control than you imagine over which pathways in your brain become strong and which ones become weak. This applies to behaviors as well, both shy and assertive ones. Each time we don't speak up, we are strengthening the neural pathways in the brain that keep us shy. That means you can also strengthen the neural pathways that make you more assertive, by learning and practicing over time, using appropriate strategies and techniques.

●●●

Sharon Begley, science columnist for the *Wall Street Journal* writes, "If you combine the discoveries of the plasticity of the adult brain, with the hints of what underlies shyness, then I'd say one has to entertain the possibility that an adult's 'shyness circuits' can be remodeled." In short, you can always learn a few new tricks, if you want to. It's not hard work. What it takes is repetition and perseverance.

are you sure you're shy?

There are plenty of personality tests, such as the Myers-Briggs Type Indicator, that will reveal your true personality type. You may have taken one in high school, or on your first job, and earned the label of "introvert." One problem with these personality tests is that they don't tell the whole story. In the real world, you cannot be defined by a single word—there are many factors that determine your behavior. Plus, you are constantly changing. Even if you have a naturally quiet temperament, chances are there are moments, environments, or circumstances in which you are less shy, or perhaps not shy at all. Maybe you don't have a lot to say in every situation, but there are probably other times when you're quite talkative. Until now, you may have been limited by the habits you've formed. But the actions that go along with the label of shyness—such as keeping your opinions to yourself at a staff meeting or letting a new contact walk away without exchanging business cards— these are things you do, actions you take, or actions you don't take. And you can decide to take a different action in any situation.

Even if the label of "shy" reflects your natural temperament, it's likely you are capable of much more— we all are. When we believe the labels, we limit our ability to recognize how flexible we are; we fail to see how much potential each and every one of us has.

▶**try this**. Take this sentence: "I am _____." Fill in the blank using different combinations or variations. Try for 100 different ways, but feel free to do more. Do it over the course of a few days or a week as you observe yourself in action. Notice the many different aspects of yourself. See how many pages you can fill, and then study the range and expansiveness of who you are.

when are you shy?

We don't always need to understand *why* we are shy. It really doesn't matter. But if we want to expand our comfort zone, we need to know *what* we do and *when* we do it. Finding that out is as simple as observing yourself.

Instead of making a blanket statement such as "I'm shy," it makes more sense to begin to identify the situations in which you are most uncomfortable and the types of people in whose presence you feel shy. Then identify the ones that make you feel the most comfortable. That way you can create a plan to systematically expand your comfort zone.

- Are you shy in big groups but not in small ones? If so, where is the cut-off point for size?

- Are you shy around people with authority, but not around those you consider your peers?

- Is there one person or type of person around whom you're the most shy?

- Are you shy around outgoing people, or with people who seem loud and boisterous? Do you see these people as aggressive?

- Are you shy with people who are considering hiring you, but then once you've got the job, you relax and can be yourself?

- Are you shy at gatherings of people you've never met before?

- Are there settings in which you take a lesser role in something that you have been highly involved in designing, implementing, or managing?

- Do you shrug off compliments and have trouble taking credit for success?

- Are you shy around people of the opposite sex, or the same sex?

- Are you shy at any hint of conflict, or when other people are expressing their opinions freely?

- Are you shy at a particular time of day, for example in the early hours rather than in the evening?

- Are you shy if someone asks you a direct question, even when you can voluntarily offer the information any other time?

- Are you shy in formal settings, but outgoing when it's more casual?

- Are you shy when there is pressure to perform, such as speaking to a reporter or into a tape recorder? What about when there's no chance to retract what you say? Does it feels as though this is your only chance?

- Do you notice yourself saying phrases such as, "I'm sorry," or "Excuse me," but are unable to stop yourself?

Do you:

- Apologize all the time?

- Avoid potential conflict?

- Fear making a mistake?

- Find yourself annoyed and irritable in groups?

- Blame others for your discomfort?

- Get mad at yourself easily?

- Feel things are often unfair?

Reflect a bit on these lists. What is it about these situations that allow you to turn a part of yourself off? Why do you lose access to your ideas and your words? It is very natural to think of being shy as containing a large measure of victimhood. But if you think about it, it is actually selfish to be shy. Not only are we withholding our ideas from others, but we require special attention and additional time to feel comfortable. That's not always possible. We do have something of value to offer and it's not fair to others—in fact, it's stingy of us not to contribute just because we don't feel like it.

what are your fears?

The problem with our fears is that they are locked in our heads. This may be a great thing! If the fears are all in our heads, we have complete control over them—if we accept the fears as the destructive forces they are, instead of mistaking them for some kind of reality. If we can bring the fears out into the open, they can be examined, and we can decide whether or not the fears correspond to reality.

● ● ●

Let's go back to Kathy, who is terrified of attending a networking event because she doesn't know what to say to a stranger:

"I'm afraid I will say the wrong thing, or I will mumble or not finish a complete sentence, and the other person will be looking at me as though I'm stupid." So the way she tells it, Kathy is afraid of the way someone will look at her. Is that something to fear?

"Okay, let's say someone looks at you as though you're stupid. Then what will happen?"

"Well, the other person will reject me."

"How, exactly?"

"Well, he will just walk away in disgust."

"Has that ever happened to you before?"

"No, not really."

"Have you ever seen someone do that?"

"Well, no."

"And have you ever done it to someone?"

"No, I would never do that."

"So here's the picture: You introduce yourself to a stranger and at first he is interested in what you have to say, but as soon as you start to stutter or say something 'stupid' this person gets fed up, rolls his eyes, and walks away in disgust? Do you really think that would happen?"

●●●

As the picture of what Kathy imagines gets filled in with details, she can start to see how irrational and how unlikely it is. And yet, when the fear is inside her head, it seems completely plausible — so plausible that she has convinced herself not to attend an event because of it.

That's only one fear — there are many more where that one came from. What about the fear of confrontation, of being humiliated, of not knowing the answer, or of being judged by authority figures such as bosses, supervisors, clients, and prospects? If we look objectively at our own fears, especially the tiny ones that hide behind automatic reactions, we may see that they are just as unrealistic as Kathy's. Sometimes looking at the fears helps just enough to aid us in overcoming them.

▶ **try this**. Next time you notice that a fear is holding you back, write out the scene of what you imagine will happen. This will help you see whether it is realistic or not. Show what you've written to someone you trust; ask his or her opinion. Sometimes a second opinion is enough of a motivator to let go of a fear.

what you feel isn't the most important thing

Western culture places tremendous value on feelings. We are encouraged to get in touch with our feelings, to work on our feelings, to think and talk about our feelings, and to treat our feelings with the utmost respect and attention, as if they were our most valuable asset. We are encouraged to steer clear of anything uncomfortable. We do what's easiest or most familiar instead of what needs to be done. We choose activities and events based on personal interest or entertainment value. We rarely do anything we don't feel like doing. This is how many of us make our decisions, both trivial and important ones, from making a difficult phone call to choosing a career.

> *We are not out of touch with our inner world— that world of feelings, of preferences, of desires and discomfort. It is a world we know too well. In the course of exploring our pain, our worries, our feelings and our dreams we forego the development of our more needed skill—to notice and engage the world around us."*
> —Gregg Krech, author
> *Naikan: Gratitude, Grace and the Japanese Art of Self-Reflection*

We believe that getting what we want should be easy. We are seduced by hyperbolic promises such as "Become self-confident in 10 days," or "Get fit without doing exercise." These voices are speaking to the part of us that wants to feel good and doesn't want to work, to the part of us that engages in magical thinking. But most of us know that mastery in life happens slowly through time, and only with great effort. If a goal is worth striving toward, it usually requires work, sacrifice, and often discomfort. So are our feelings really the best foundation for decision-making?

Think about the networking meeting that Kathy is afraid to attend. What if one of her goals is to build her business and bring in enough work so she can hire an employee and spend more time with her family? She knows that networking is an essential tool in that process, but she is terrified of talking to strangers and therefore never feels interested in going anywhere new.

Can Kathy stop the fear through sheer force of will? Probably not. But if she allows her feelings to prevent her from doing what's needed to achieve her goals, then she won't build her business and she won't be able to hire that new employee and fulfill her dreams. Goals aren't achieved by magic. No amount of wishful thinking, feeling good, or dreaming will grow your business or help you climb the corporate ladder. If your long-term goals are important to you, whatever they are, you'll no doubt have to endure some discomfort to achieve them. That's a given. Having a different attitude might help get through that discomfort. It would be more constructive to place less value on how we feel and more value on our goals and what we're trying to accomplish, both professionally and personally.

where is your attention?

Andy gave feedback on a report to a coworker, who seemed appreciative of it. But not long afterward, he started to imagine that he'd been too harsh and worried that the coworker was angry with him.

●●●

Many of us spend time imagining what has happened or what will happen. Think about how often you catch yourself replaying an awkward conversation in your head or rehearsing what you'll say when you talk to your boss. When this is going on, where is your attention? It may seem as though your attention is focused outward because these thoughts have to do with someone else. But in fact your attention is focused inward, on yourself and what you imagine others will think of you. In reality, you have no idea what another person thinks, much less what someone will say or do. You will never know. You can get some information by watching and listening, but when your attention is focused inward, it's impossible to see or hear. You miss offhand comments or body language that could help you read the other person more accurately; you miss openings that could get you closer to your goal.

Morita Therapy, founded by the Japanese psychiatrist Shoma Morita, teaches acceptance of our feelings while shifting our attention to something more constructive. It is based on the idea that we can make a conscious attempt to shift attention from our feelings to our purpose. "We focus our attention on the things that help us live a fulfilled and meaningful life," writes Morita. "We don't allow our anxiety to prevent us from taking the actions that will lead us toward our goals. We simply bring the anxiety along as we strive to live well and do what's important." This is simple, but not necessarily easy. It means you have to notice where your attention is first, and then redirect it.

For example, if you're sitting in a meeting, rehearsing what you'll say when it's your turn to speak and not paying attention to the comments that come before you, your focus is inward. In those moments, you can catch yourself and redirect your attention to the people in the room. You will likely hear or see something new—something that could affect what you will say—something that could trigger a brilliant new idea.

This is just the tip of the iceberg of what you may be missing. Action can pull you back into reality and distract you from your shyness. The shyness doesn't disappear; it just moves out of the spotlight and becomes less of an obstacle. Paradoxically, the more action you take, the less shy you will feel. As David Reynolds writes in *Constructive Living*, "Not only will you become more skillful and confident in work situations by gaining experience in them, but you will be turning more and more attention away from yourself (and your problems) toward the reality out there." You become a shy person who speaks up and reaches out.

Paths to Developing Self-Confidence

Brenda is a manager at a publishing company. She wants to have her own retail store, but she doesn't "believe in herself" enough to make that leap. She's taken several steps to set the foundation for her own business, but can't seem to finalize her plans, and she doesn't know why. She thinks it has to do with a lack of confidence. "I don't truly believe I can make this happen. I think it could happen, but my attitude is full of fear. All I can think of are reasons why it won't work—it's such a saturated market—and I know these thoughts will weaken me."

Brenda seems to believe that she needs self-confidence—which she thinks other people have plenty of—before she takes the plunge. This logic suggests that having confidence is somehow a prerequisite to effort and success. But it's a catch-22 situation, because unless Brenda has this elusive self-confidence, she won't believe she's capable of succeeding, and so she won't make her best effort. Indeed, many people make no effort at all, using their lack of confidence as an excuse.

But is self-confidence required to take action? Can taking an action result in the confidence needed to take another action? In other words, which comes first: self-confidence or action toward a goal? If you believe that self-confidence comes first, you will be waiting passively for a very long time. And during that time, you'll probably succeed only in convincing yourself that there's nothing you can do.

But if you believe that action comes first, whether you feel confident or not, then there's nothing to wait for. That's when you understand that practically everything that happens to you is a direct (or indirect) result of the actions you take. When you take action first, you realize that you are responsible for what comes next, and that you are in a position not to control, but rather to shape the outcome of your life.

David Reynolds, author of *Constructive Living*, writes that "feelings wag the tail of behavior." In other words, we can influence our feelings through our behavior. If you extend your hand feebly when meeting someone new, you're likely to feel timid. If, on the other hand, you extend your hand confidently, you will begin to experience a shift in your feelings, which you can build on by continuing the behavior. You will be affected by the response of others as well. A confident handshake begets a smile, and so on.

The suggestion is that confidence comes as a direct result, not of success, but of effort. It goes like this: (1) you take action; (2) that action has an effect; and (3) you learn something from the effect. You try again; something else results; you learn something else. You should take every opportunity that comes your way and use it as part of your continuous, lifelong experiment.

Confidence is a by-product of effort, which doesn't mean the confident person does everything (or anything) perfectly. It means that you've given your best effort at that moment in time. And if you continue to do what needs to be done to the best of your ability, learning from each effort—every mistake and every success—you will become more competent and increasingly self-confident. In that gradual progression from self-conscious to self-confident, you nurture your own confidence by learning from all your experiences. Your attention will become less and less focused on yourself and your lack of confidence.

Here's another way of looking at it: If self-consciousness or anxiety is a big rock that gets in your way, then self-confidence simply requires that you move the rock. With the obstacle removed, you can do what needs to be done. Your attention will be on the task at hand, not on yourself or any feelings you have. Accept the facts and your feelings as they are now. Don't let them stop you from doing what you need to do. So even if your heart is pounding so loud you can barely hear yourself speak, let your boss know that telling you once is sufficient, and you don't need to be reminded.

3 simple steps to overcome shyness

The point is not to overcome the shyness itself, but to overcome the interference of shyness in your daily life. We're all guilty of avoiding the tasks we don't enjoy or do well, letting our feelings guide our decisions about what to do and how to spend our time. That's why we may need a little reminder about the three simple things required to overcome shyness:

1. self-awareness. First, you must be able to see and recognize that you are doing something and then examine what you are doing, especially in situations that typically present a problem for you. Watch your habitual behavior and be ready to interrupt it.

2. desire to do different. It's simple to make a decision to speak up, but it's not always as simple to keep the commitment. Habits such as keeping quiet are well-worn paths that are easy to tread. Think of these new activities as a rocky, untrodden path. It may hurt your feet a bit, but if you stay on the path, your feet will toughen up, your muscles for climbing will strengthen, and eventually you will reach the peak.

3. self-discipline and willpower. Overcoming shyness is all about taking life one day at a time. Don't bite off more than you can chew. Don't look too far ahead, or perceive the task as bigger than it is. Simply take one action at a time. Each and every time you want to wander back to that old, comfortable path, pause for a moment and decide again what you want. Remind yourself of your goal.

5 steps to changing your habits

If Kathy, for example, wanted to change her habit of finding any excuse not to attend an event, she would:

1. Notice or identify the habit.

2. Have a desire to change the habit.

3. Commit to be alert. Notice when the behavior starts.

4. Do something different in that moment.

5. Repeat the steps throughout her day.

Here's how it might sound in Kathy's head:

"I don't want to go to that meeting. It's raining and it's far away and I probably won't know anyone there. The people are going to be boring anyway." But as soon as this voice starts, Kathy says to herself, *"No matter what ingenious excuse I come up with, I'm not going to give in. That's an old familiar voice that reinforces my old habits and old outcomes, and I always feel bad when I succumb to it. If I want something different to happen today, I must do something different today. I know I want to grow my business and have an employee hired by this time next year so I can spend more time with my family. That's why I will go to that meeting."*

7 ways to develop your own self-confidence

There is an abundance of books and classes offering confidence-building tips to the legions of seekers who hope to get rid of their of low self-esteem. Techniques abound to help you inject confidence into every aspect of your life, with virtually no effort on your part. Unfortunately, none of them work. That short-term, pump-me-up, "I've got a big meeting tomorrow," type of confidence is like cramming for a test the night before, only to forget the material once the test is over. Your confidence deflates the minute the meeting is over because it's not anchored in any ongoing experience or learning curve.

In the real world, there is no quick fix. Self-confidence is not something you either have or don't have. You can't buy self-confidence on-line. You'll never turn off the TV and feel more confident. You won't wake up tomorrow a changed person. The only kind of confidence you can actually build is one based on effort and competence. As with all useful skills, self-confidence is developed through training and practice. So how do you start building confidence? Here are a few ideas:

1. stop comparing yourself to others. We all evaluate ourselves in relation to others. The problem is you have no idea what the motivating factors are behind another person's actions. You can't know why they do what they do. In fact, someone who looks confident may just be another shy person covering up his or her own insecurities and doubts.

2. set self-confidence goals. Although developing self-confidence can be an abstract goal, and self-confidence itself is impossible to quantify, you can focus on the tangible and concrete actions that result in confidence. Try choosing one area and break it down into small, manageable steps or actions that have concrete results. Make your goals measurable, such as "Strike up a conversation with one stranger per day," "Call three headhunters," or "Attend two events per month." Write down your goals and post them somewhere visible, such as the bathroom mirror or on your computer. Review your goals every morning, or at least every week. Over time, and with persistence, you'll be a shy person who starts conversations.

3. always take time to prepare. Don't waste time talking yourself into feeling confident. Be more productive in your preparation. The better you know your stuff, the more confident you will feel. No matter what the event or activity, make sure you set aside time to practice or think through all the possible scenarios and how you would respond to them. Again, it's a question of directing your attention away from the anxiety and toward the actions needed to accomplish your goals.

4. visualize another reality. Before a stressful event, take a few minutes to create a mental picture for yourself. Instead of imagining a staff meeting as a place where you will be put on the spit and grilled, imagine it as a circle of colleagues who are all there to help you. Instead of picturing the company holiday party as a mob scene where everyone will be in their cliques and you'll be alone in the corner, think about it as a series of one-on-one conversations over a glass of your favorite wine.

5. ask for honest feedback. It might seem counterintuitive to submit yourself to the scrutiny of others, but you may be surprised by what you find out. It's likely that your perspective on yourself isn't accurate, and it's definitely not complete. The only way to discover the big picture is to submit yourself or your work to someone else's opinion. Solicit honest feedback from someone you trust. Sometimes all you have to do is ask. This isn't to say that what others say about you is always the truth, but your own opinion is a very narrow slice of the pie. You need more information, and more perspectives, to weigh the situation correctly.

6. think small. It's unrealistic to imagine that you will suddenly transform yourself into a gregarious networker. But you can get in the habit of doing tiny, confident behaviors, of stretching yourself and expanding your comfort zone. For example, when you meet someone for the first time, greet him or her with a firm handshake, a smile, and look directly into his or her eyes for a moment longer than may be comfortable. Or, when talking on the phone, smile. The person on the other end can hear it and will respond to the energy in your voice. If you want an enthusiastic response to your ideas, bring that enthusiasm into your voice.

7. give yourself options. One of the reasons we get so nervous about one conversation, one interview, or one prospect is because we don't have a lot of eggs in our basket, so every egg counts for a great deal. If you give yourself more options, and more opportunities to practice saying the things that need to be said, not only will it get easier, but each egg won't carry as much weight. You'll be able to afford a few unsuccessful conversations because you know there will be more opportunities in the future.

●●●

With every moment of confidence, your momentum will build. The more confidence you develop, the less clutter you'll have in your mind. The more you can open your mind to what others have to say, the more you will become a genuinely curious person.

Curiosity is the antidote to shyness. The simple process of asking questions is the catalyst that allows you to redirect your attention. Curiosity takes your attention away from yourself (and what you imagine others are thinking about you) and puts it on another person. It is thanks to curiosity, and the open mind required to be curious, that we are able to learn the things that take us to the next stage in our careers and our lives.

Self-confidence is not a form of arrogance. It is trust in our capacity to awaken. It is both the courage to face whatever life throws at us without losing equanimity, and the humility to treat every situation we encounter as one from which we can learn."

—Steven Batchelor, author
Buddhism Without Beliefs

3

Overcome Fears With Curiosity

Everyone tells Andy he is a good listener. He is often perceived as an especially good listener because he doesn't say much. And he doesn't say much because he's shy, or so he says. In truth, Andy doesn't speak up because he doesn't want to sound stupid. He dreads talking to strangers or chiming in with his opinion in a group discussion because he's afraid he'll say the wrong thing and everyone will laugh. In a one-on-one conversation he can't stand any awkward silence, because he's positive the other person thinks he's a complete bore.

Clearly, Andy is listening to something, but most of it is going on in his own mind. If he didn't consider himself shy, he wouldn't be so self-conscious about what he says and how he imagines it will sound. If he didn't see himself as shy, maybe he'd contribute a thought or an idea to a conversation. But Andy can't do that unless he listens to what's going on in the real world, not what's inside his head.

learning to listen

Listening is such a simple act. It requires us to be attentive, but we don't have to do anything else. We needn't advise, coach, or even sound wise. All we have to do is sit and listen. You've probably had the experience of speaking with someone who says "uh huh" in all the right places, but then makes a comment proving they didn't hear a word you said. In fact, many people listen that way, automatically, not expecting anything new or extraordinary to come out of the conversation. Does any of this happen when you think you're listening?

- You are bored by what you're hearing.
- You're waiting for the speaker to stop speaking so you can talk.
- You rehearse your response, your opinion, or your story to top the one being told.
- You mechanically repeat the same things you always say.
- You judge the other person, or what he or she is saying.
- You label and stereotype, saying "He's such a liberal," "She's so California."
- You pretend to agree (rather than ask what is meant) when you don't recognize a word or phrase.
- You compare yourself to the other person.

With all of this going on, how could you possibly be listening? There's no space to take in anything new, no room for curiosity.

being curious instead of certain

What if you were curious about the world instead of certain about what it has to offer? To become curious means to stop for a moment and remember that there are other people in the world, and that if we open our minds for a moment, we might learn something we didn't know or discover something we weren't aware of, or make a connection we would have otherwise missed. But it's exactly that unknown factor that makes us so nervous.

Andy doesn't like not understanding what his boss is saying, and he doesn't want his boss to see that he doesn't understand, so his mind wanders off as he starts to imagine what his boss must be thinking and Andy misses what his boss says! It may be an offhand compliment or a subtle suggestion or a one-time offer. But he missed it. If Andy can't tolerate the uncomfortable feeling of not knowing, then he cannot be curious, because curiosity—by definition—requires that we admit we don't know something. So how do we develop the genuine curiosity—a real desire to know—that inspires relevant and insightful questions that can take a conversation anywhere? How do we develop an inquisitive mind if we don't already have one?

▶ **try this.** First, prepare yourself for slight discomfort. Then begin a conversation with someone who thinks differently than you do. Instead of listening for what you have in common, your task is to listen for anything different, anything that surprises you. Stop the voice of judgment or opinion. Just listen. Notice when words are used that you don't understand. If a question comes to mind, ask it. If not, just keep listening. At the end of the conversation, notice whether the discomfort stayed the same throughout or whether it subsided at any point. Notice whether you learned anything new. (Adapted from the writings of Margaret Wheatley.)

6 ways to develop your listening skills

1. be open. These are two little words, but it's such a huge task! Being open means forgetting everything you know about the person or the topic, and listening with every sense you have.

2. don't be distracted. Give your full attention to the conversation. Don't let your eyes wander if someone enters the room or passes by. Don't answer your phone. Don't scratch an itch. These are all signals to the other person that the conversation isn't important.

3. be active. Listening seems passive because you're just sitting there and no visible action is required. But listening is actually quite active. Let ideas and thoughts play in your mind. Don't hesitate to jump into the conversation.

4. don't interrupt. Resist the urge to say what you have to say as soon as it occurs to you. Make a note of your pressing thought if you need to, but don't speak for the sake of speaking, or because you finally came up with something good. This won't add to the conversation. It's more likely to derail it.

5. reveal yourself. If you're quiet by nature, you've probably been "accused" at one point or another of not saying anything about yourself. That's one of the dangers of being quiet. But being a good listener doesn't mean all you do is listen. A good listener also reveals information about him or herself that makes the other person feel more comfortable about opening up.

6. ask unexpected questions. Don't ask a question you think you know the answer to. Use unexpected questions to find out what makes the other person tick. You may get an unexpected response, that will take you on a different path.

" *We have the opportunity many times a day, everyday, to be the one who listens to others, curious rather than certain. And the greatest benefit that comes to those who listen is that we develop closer relationships with those we thought we couldn't understand. When we listen with less judgment, we always develop a better relationship with each other. It's not differences that divide us. It's our judgments that do. Curiosity and good listening bring us back together."*

—Margaret Wheatley
Shambhala Sun, November 2001

how to read other people

Listening isn't only about hearing someone's words. It also requires the ability to read other people—to understand how to perceive and interpret patterns of actions, gestures, comments, vocal inflections, and more. This skill is essential to succeeding in business, because if we can't read other people, we are likely to misjudge a boss's intentions, misread a colleague's actions, or mishear a client's request.

Reading other people has nothing to do with approving or disapproving, or with your opinions of what you interpret. You can't evaluate others based on your own personal value system or you won't learn anything about them. Instead, you must learn to measure the behavior of others by what is appropriate for the situation. But first we must see other people, and that isn't as easy as it sounds. Because we're human, our feelings cloud our perceptions. On top of that, preconceptions, prejudices, desires, and cultural conditioning prevent us from seeing clearly and assessing situations accurately. We perceive things the way we imagine them and rarely the way they actually are. We imagine everyone is just like us, when they're not.

●●●

Andy is a perfectionist, so he assumes his boss is too. He believes that his boss wants him to be perfect. That may not be true. His boss may want to be admired. His boss may want him to make mistakes so he can reprimand him. If Andy could see his boss clearly, he might not worry so much about being perfect.

●●●

Brenda needs a lot of encouragement, so she assumes others do too. When her coworkers are collaborating on a project, instead of giving honest feedback to get it right, she plays the role of cheerleader, because that's what she would want in that situation.

●●●

In an excellent book on this topic, *Reading People,* Dr. Jo-Ellan Dimitrius describes the basic skills needed to master what she calls "the lost art of reading people." Here are a few:

- Spend more time with people in order to learn to understand them.

- Stop, look, and listen. Be patient and attentive. Practice watching and listening with all of your senses.

- Learn to reveal something of yourself. To get others to open up, you must first open up to them. This establishes a foundation of trust.

To read people accurately, you also must be objective. If you can be aware of what gets in the way of being objective, you have a better chance of seeing clearly. There are four states of mind that most often lead to a loss of objectivity:

1. emotional commitment. The desire to keep everyone happy and avoid confrontation may cause you to misread others. If you choose a friend as your business partner, your emotional commitment may cause you to overlook unacceptable performance. You may neglect taking action to address it. (Strategy: Get someone else to give you an objective perspective before making a decision.)

2. neediness. If you agree to do a project or take on a client because you need the money, you may ignore, or simply not see, the red flags indicating that they may be difficult to work with. (Strategy: Take enough time to make a proper decision and explore other options.)

3. fear. Fear of being fired by a client or an employer can cause you to mishear or misinterpret what they say. (Strategy: Make lists of the fears and consequences to help you see them more objectively, and evaluate whether they are realistic.)

4. defensiveness. If you are being criticized by a customer or colleague, it's virtually impossible to hear what they are saying without giving in to the impulse to defend yourself. (Strategy: Stay as silent as you possibly can and know that you will be able to respond later.)

●●●

Reading other people involves recognizing and interpreting nonverbal signals and cues, including gestures, facial expressions, body language, and more. Something as simple as how a person sits or stands can help you understand what they're saying. A secretive or anxious person will keep his or her distance physically, glance down or look away when addressed, and may have a weak handshake. A person who stands with his or her arms crossed protectively across the chest is often defensive. And a person who stands in the classical "figleaf" stance, with hands crossed in front at waist level, may be timid or weak.

The face, with 43 muscle groups, can reveal more than most of us are aware of. A flushed face and averted glance can indicate embarrassment, but sometimes also anger. Clenched teeth or jaw (or any stiffness in the body) hints at defensiveness. Even a person's breathing can reveal his or her state of mind. Are he or she breathing deeply and in a relaxed way? Are his or her breaths short and shallow?

An advanced skill is the ability to read people while you are speaking, so you can moderate how you are coming across and determine when it is time to end a conversation. To do this, you must learn to focus both outward and inward simultaneously. Here are three things you should be aware of when reading people:

1. body language. Rolling eyes, or signs of boredom or attentiveness? Moving toward you or away from you?

2. tone of the exchange. Are there awkward pauses or silences? Loss of interest? Noises and whispering?

3. self-disclosure. Is the other person pulling back or giving more?

When someone is ready to end a conversation, certain actions telegraph that readiness. Getting up is a pretty clear sign, but others include glancing at a clock or at the door, straightening papers on a desk, or even something as subtle as putting a cap on a pen. These may be conscious or unconscious, but they are worth paying attention to if you don't want to overstay your welcome.

Reading others also includes getting to know the other person over time and watching for patterns. One of the benefits of getting to know colleagues with whom you work every day is that you recognize certain traits and signals of distress or problems early on, and can address them before things escalate. You can ask a question, make an observation, or offer a suggestion to avoid a problem.

The distractions that prevent us from listening also prevent us from seeing other people clearly and reading them accurately. But if we change the focus, we'll have a much clearer picture of reality, and we'll be able to respond accordingly.

" " *You can make more friends in two months by becoming interested in other people than you can in two years trying to get other people interested in you."*

—Dale Carnegie

Skills and Strategies for Shy People

Network Your Way

Jack is the CEO of a small furniture company. He started his business in his garage and it has since grown to employ more than 25 people. Jack claims to be a shy person, but he knws the importance of networking. As much as he dislikes it, he forces himself to do the schmoozing and glad-handing required to bring in enough business to support his company and his employees. The problem is that he could never walk into a room and just casually meet people. After all these years, he still can't do it! But Jack needed to find a way to make this scenario a reality, so he devised a strategy. Jack gives himself a task, does the task, and then goes home. For example, he sets to goal of meeting three people. So he finds his three people, he introduces himself, hands over his business card, chats a bit, and then moves on. Once he meets his goal, he can go home.

●●●

Networking is a combination of two simple things:

- An open and generous attitude toward other people.

- An awareness of all the tiny efforts you could make to constantly expand your network and deepen your relationships.

For example, when you attend an industry event or conference, what do you write on your name tag? If you are reluctant to initiate conversations, then it's your job to extend silent invitations to others. Your name tag can help you do that. If all you write is your name—no company name, no title, no information about what you do or who you work for—you aren't giving other attendees anything to work with.

Think a moment before you decide what to write. Where are you? Who are the people you'll be meeting? Is your company name familiar? If you give your official title, will it mean anything to them? If you have your own company and the name isn't recognizable yet, your tagline may be a good thing to include. Decide which details to include, but don't include too many—it's a small space. What you put on your name tag could provoke enough interest that others approach you and initiate a conversation, so you won't have to. It's a small thing, but has a big impact.

Here's another scenario: You are at a conference luncheon. You hate crowds. You're sitting with a bunch of strangers. They're not talking to you; you're not talking to them. You would, but you can't think of anything to say. How much longer do you have to sit there? Could it get any worse?

●●●

Where is your attention? If this scenario at all resembles what's in your mind, your attention is squarely on yourself and how you feel. You have so many other options. Open your eyes. Have you looked around the table to see who's there? You'll probably see some people talking to each other, others sitting silently. This is a perfect opportunity. Direct your attention to their name tags. Are there any familiar names or company names? If no one's wearing name tags, have you noticed who's smiling, or who's grimacing and maybe feeling the same way you are? Are there any other shy people in the room? Watch the quiet ones for a little bit and see if you can read them.

Next, choose someone to talk to. It could be the person closest to you. That's easiest. Or choose someone randomly, because you never know where a conversation will lead. Now, before you start worrying about what to say, think instead about what questions you could ask. "What's your interest in software development?" (or whatever the topic is) always gets to the heart of things and bypasses a lot of chitchat. It's a simple question, but could be just the right jumping off point for a conversation. Many people who attend a networking event wait for the networking to happen to them and don't initiate conversations. If this is your tendency, catch it early and do something different.

don't expect to feel comfortable at first

In the beginning, don't expect to feel comfortable doing this, but don't let those feelings push you around. Remember that what you feel is not the most important thing, and that it's constantly changing anyway, so even if you don't feel like it right now, you may in a little while. In fact, forcing yourself to reach out even when you don't feel like it can change your mood drastically. If you dive into the conversation, you may get so involved that you'll forget how you feel.

Remember also that your goals—making new contacts for your career or for growing your business—are more important, and you've already accepted the fact that you may have to do some uncomfortable things to achieve them.

think about other people

We're so used to thinking about ourselves—so focused on what we want and how we're going to get it—that turning the focus outward will take time before it becomes a habit. It can be a total mindshift, but the defined context of a networking event helps when it has a beginning, a middle, and an end. These types of events are great places to practice your networking skills. And it helps to observe other people and assess their attitude.

Next time you're at an event, see if you can identify the good networkers and watch what they do. They won't necessarily be the most outgoing people there. It could be the woman sitting quietly with another, deep in conversation. Or it could be the man scribbling notes on the back of a business card. Or it could be the guy who drags a colleague across the room to meet someone else.

Find the good networkers and look for these qualities:

enthusiastic. They are positive and interested.

resourceful. They are bubbling with ideas and taking time to make connections for people.

generous. They share information and resources, and help others to get what they need.

open. They are looking for help, asking for what they need, and receiving ideas and assistance graciously and humbly.

curious. They are genuinely curious and genuinely engaged in the conversation.

●●●

You're not trying to transform your attitude completely, you're just experimenting with one specific attitude during certain activities. (Although if you extend this attitude into other areas of your life, it couldn't hurt.) Even if your knees are shaking and you are sure you'll make a fool of yourself, remember that what you imagine is rarely comparable to the actual experience. And once you're talking to people, it's not that painful. You might even leave thinking, "That wasn't so bad."

set simple networking goals

Because networking isn't something you're eager to do, it makes sense to set up a structure to help you do it. For example, rather than waiting until an event comes along, use the following questions to determine your networking goals for the type of events you want to attend:

- What is the next step for your career? Find someone who is already in that position and see if you know anyone who knows that person.

- What do you want to learn about? Find a group or two that holds educational events on this topic and get on its mailing list.

● Who do you want to meet? Keep your eyes open for events where these types of people will be speaking. Or even schedule a Google news alert with their names so you'll be notified of any press releases or other news items with their names.

●●●

Commit to attending X events per month, and then actively look for the best events to fill those slots. X can be a number that grows as you go along. Start with one event per month as a minimum. Then, once you've got that under your belt, move up to two. And if more than two events happen to be occurring in the same month, don't use your goal as a limit. Attend as many as you can fit into your schedule.

You might soon find that you no longer need your goals and are hearing about events right and left. Perhaps you've joined one of the groups and your involvement means you are expected at a certain number of meetings.

It also helps to have a purpose when networking, a cause to champion, a project to organize, or even a question to get answered. Anything that gets people excited and gives them a reason to talk to you.

Jack could go with the purpose of meeting other small business owners to see if they are interested in forming a small group where they can share resources and inspire each other in a noncompetitive environment. This would make starting conversations much easier. And he might not feel the need to go home quite so soon.

networking techniques for shy people

You will succeed at networking—and in business—if you approach it with a positive and measured attitude. Instead of being overwhelmed by everything you could be doing, focus on the few tiny and manageable efforts you can make, such as choosing the right events to attend, taking time to prepare before you show up, or simply making sure you have your business cards in the jacket or bag you're bringing along.

choosing the right event to attend

The point is simply to get out, learn something new, and meet some new people in the process. So instead of choosing events based on your personal interest in the topic, think about which events will attract the people who can help you achieve your goals. Here are a few questions to help you make those decisions:

What level of businessperson does the topic attract? Executives? Mid-level managers? Is it a technical topic? Is the event focused on networking or is it educational? Does the topic address an issue you or your customers face? If so, then go. And bring back some ideas for them.

Do you want to meet the speakers? If so, then go. And be sure to introduce yourself at the end, get their business card, and follow up later with "I heard you speak." To get a dialogue going, refer to something he or she said that had an impact on you. Or ask a question you didn't have the opportunity to ask at the event.

Does the event relate to a new idea you haven't had time to focus on? If so, then go. Use it as a catalyst to start focusing your goals.

preparing for an event

There is nothing better than preparation to make you feel comfortable. And there is a lot of preparation you can do for networking so that when you arrive at an event, you are ready to be open.

find out who'll be there. For a conference, or even a monthly event, see if the list of attendees is available—sometimes it is published as part of the event's marketing. If not, it's worth a call to the organizers to find out if it's available. Then go through the list and note those you'd like to meet.

Keep the list with you during the event and keep track of whom you've met and whom you still need to meet. (For advanced networking, join a group and volunteer to be one of the meeting coordinators, which will give you access to this information.)

do your research. Whether or not you can get the list of attendees, you'll always know who the speakers will be. If there are some you'd like to meet, do a little intelligence gathering on the Internet to prepare for a conversation with them.

Focus especially on what you can find out about their business and personal interests, and think about how you might be able to help them. And don't keep your research a secret. When you meet the contact, say, "I always make a special effort to inquire about the people I'd like to meet." Inevitably, people are flattered. Wouldn't you be?

the first few minutes are the hardest

The most challenging part of networking is getting started, so here is a play-by-play scenario of the beginning of an event, and some tiny efforts to keep in mind that will distract you from your feelings and get you into the action.

First of all, arrive early. If you wait until most of the attendees are there, it will seem as though everyone is already engaged in conversation, and it won't be as easy to find your way in. By arriving early, you can greet others as they arrive and engage them in conversation before they find someone else to talk to.

What do you do first? Sign in, pay your money, and get your name tag, right? Instead of trying to get away with as little interaction as possible, start connecting right away with the person at the registration desk. Introduce yourself and let him or her know this is your first event. This person is likely to be very involved in the group. He or she will want you to feel comfortable so she might hand you off to someone who will introduce you around.

If you make your first interaction a positive one, it will make the next one that much easier. It could very well be smooth sailing from that moment on, all because of that one interaction you initiated with the very first person you saw. As for where to put your name tag, there's no right place. Some say the right lapel is best because people read from left to right. Others argue for placing it on the left so that, if you're shaking hands with your right, they'll have a clear line of sight to your nametag. Wherever you place it, just make sure it's easy to read.

entering the room

If you arrive early at an event, you may notice people scattered around the room, one lone person in each row of chairs or at each table. Instead of doing the same, choose one person, approach and say, "Do you mind if I join you?" Then introduce yourself and you're off into conversation land.

If it's a presentation where you may have a chance to ask questions, sit near the front. That way the presenter is more likely to call on you, and you may even have a chance to tell the group who you are and what you do. That's a good thing because there may be someone in the room who needs to talk to you and doesn't even know it!

If it's a buffet reception, stand by the food and use it to start conversations. "The shrimp is delicious." Then make it your business to move around so you can meet as many people as possible.

It sometimes helps to attend an event with a friend or colleague. You can ease your way in by approaching the first few people together. Then split up to meet people on your own. Many opportunities to make new contacts are lost because people sit with their cohorts, or with the same safe buddies every time. It's easy to stay clumped together, which discourages others from approaching you. Even if it's uncomfortable at first, make it a habit to sit with people you don't know. And if one of your important clients or contacts is at the meeting, sit with him or her, but make sure you are seated at the table with strangers also.

If you are with a business partner, there is a strategy you and your colleague can use to meet new people together. Approach someone and say, "Have you met Sally? She works for Acme Siding, and her sales this year have been amazing!" It is easier to brag about your friend as a way to introduce her, and being introduced by someone else makes conversation easier.

be one of the hosts

Once you've started attending a particular meeting regularly and you feel comfortable, take a more active role as one of the hosts. All you have to do is stand near the door and greet people as they walk in, making them feel comfortable and welcome. Or if you're at a table with others, designate yourself table moderator and suggest that everyone introduce themselves and exchange business cards.

identifying the easiest people to talk to

How do you know the right people to approach? There might be a lot of people and you want to choose wisely. You can:

look for wallflowers. Instead of trying to break into conversations that are already in progress, find someone who is sitting or standing alone and simply introduce yourself. Do it even if he looks as though he doesn't want to be approached. The outward standoffishness may merely be a cover for discomfort.

look for people who are open. Most events attract people who want to be there, so it shouldn't be hard to find people to talk to. Look for people who are looking for you. They may smile when they catch your eye. They may even approach you and introduce themselves, if you allow them to catch your eye. So keep your head up and look around the room. You're bound to see someone who is waiting for you.

ask for introductions. If you see someone you'd like to meet, don't stand there wishing they would come up to you. Ask one of the group's members (or even the director of the group) to introduce you. Don't hesitate to do the same if you notice that someone you'd like to meet is scheduled to attend.

how to join a conversation

Sometimes it may seem as though everyone is already in a conversation and no one is available to talk to you. What should you do? Join in. While in other environments this may not be appropriate, but in a networking environment, it is expected. Whether people are standing around chatting, or sitting around a table, you can join in.

Look for a physical opening. If there is a chair available, sit down, smile, and listen to the person who is speaking. Generally, people will acknowledge your presence without interrupting the speaker. You want to be both unobtrusive and present, so that when there is a conversational opening, you can speak up, introduce yourself, and become part of the conversation. When there's a break in the conversation, say, "May I join you?" or "This looked like a lively conversation so I thought I'd join in."

forgetting names

Are you one of those who says, "I can't remember names," as if it's genetic? Well, remembering names is another small effort that has a huge impact on others. Here's another opportunity to see yourself differently—as someone who remembers—and to redirect your attention during those chaotic moments of meeting someone new.

Think about it. When you first meet someone, there is so much vying for your attention: what they look like, what they're saying, the activity around you, and much more. When the person reaches out to shake your hand, it's not that you don't remember the name; you actually don't hear it. There's too much going on, both inside and out.

The moment to focus on, then, is the one in which you will hear the name. You must consciously stop your mind, take a moment, and direct your full attention. Once you've done that, the hard part is over. You can repeat the name back, if that will help. "You say your name is Bob?" Actively using the word, rather than passively taking it in, will make it more real to you and help you remember it. Then try to use the name in your response. And if you've already forgotten, don't be embarrassed. Just ask him or her to repeat it. Make a joke out if it, if it's appropriate. "Can you believe it? Not one minute has gone by and already I've forgotten your name."

On the other hand, how important is it really that you remember someone's name? In a situation where you see someone you've met before and have forgotten his or her name, rather than try to hide it, here are a couple ways to let them know: "Your name is on the tip of my tongue." Or "You look so familiar but I just can't place you." This takes the pressure off the other person too, in case they can't remember your name either.

Or if you're uncomfortable with the confession, simply extend your hand and introduce yourself. This may prompt the other person to do the same. Acknowledge having met before and give them your name again as a reminder, showing that you don't expect them to remember either.

the business-card tango

Business cards are another tiny networking tool that most people fail to take advantage of. First of all, you have to have one and, of course, keep them with you so you can exchange them with others. You'd be surprised how many people attend a business event or conference and forget their business cards! Or they only bring two, because that's all that will fit in their business card holder. Even if you don't have a job at the moment, it's important to have a simple business card with your contact information—this makes for a much more professional first impression.

The problems with business cards come up around how to give and get them, and the words that accompany that process. For example, you may decide not to offer your card, believing that if the other person wanted it, she'd ask for it. Notice the assumption being made based on virtually no reality. Remember: If you're making assumptions about what someone else is doing, you're attention is again focused inward.

Once you've noticed the direction of your focus, you can open your eyes and ask a question. How about, "I'd love to keep in touch. May I give you my card?" Or better yet, "Let's exchange cards." That eliminates the possibility that the other person won't offer his or hers in return. You've already very gently suggested that you both do the same. At that point, you might find out that he or she forgot to bring cards and is embarrassed about it, which is why it wasn't offered earlier. Did you think of that?

None of that should stop you from exchanging contact information, which is the point of the whole exercise. It's not about the business card or whether they want you to have it. It's about agreeing that you'd both like to continue the conversation at some point, or simply stay in touch. And unless you've been offensive in some way, it's very unlikely someone would say no to that.

Business-card etiquette is different around the world. For example, when doing business in many parts of Africa and Asia, always offer a business card with your right hand. In Japan, presenting a card with two hands by the two upper corners conveys respect.

Wherever you are, treat your cards and those from others with respect. When someone hands you a card, instead of sticking it right in your pocket or pile, take a moment to look at it. Notice how it's laid out. Use the business card as a conversation tool. If there is something unusual about it—the size, the colors, the logo, the text— comment on it or ask a question. Who knows where that conversation will go.

how will they remember you?

So you've had a good conversation with a new contact and you exchanged cards and promised to stay in touch. Then you get back to your office and you suddenly think, "They won't remember me. They met so many people and

I don't think I made a strong impression." Notice the assumption being made. And if that way of thinking—irrational as it is—sounds familiar, a few techniques and a little preparation before the event will help you nip it in the bud.

wear an unusual accessory. Wear a colorful scarf or tie, or even a button (political or not) so that when you follow-up, you can remind them who you are by referring to that accessory. "I was the one with the orange scarf."

bring chocolate. Always carry some delicious dark chocolate with you. If there's a lull in the conversation, offer it to whoever you're speaking with. It's a nice treat to have and share, especially at full-day conferences with no snacks. Plus, it makes for a great follow-up: "Remember, me? I was the one with the chocolate."

the best networking opportunity

It's in line for the ladies restroom. No, seriously! There is inevitably a line for the ladies room, no matter where you are. So don't waste valuable networking time by standing there silently! Talk to whoever's in front of you or behind you, and be sure to have your business cards handy. Sorry gents, this doesn't seem to hold true for the men's room!

You see, there's no "right" way to do networking. There are many different techniques for a wide variety of situations and people. Choose the ones that make the most sense for you. As your comfort zone expands and you become accustomed to the back and forth of dialog and relationship building, you will use different networking tools and strategies that weren't comfortable before, but somehow suddenly are, because you have changed, perhaps without even noticing it.

networking checklist

Beyond the research you've done, use this checklist to complete your preparation for a networking event:

- **business cards.** Bring plenty of them, more than you think you need.
- **brochures.** It's always great to hand out a professional brochure with pictures or testimonials about your company or service.
- **a pen or two.** Keep one for yourself, and lend the other one to people who aren't as prepared as you are!
- **a pad to jot notes.** Remember to write down things that pop into your head for later follow up.
- **a memorable object.** If you have chocolate, a colorful tie or scarf, or buttons, you can refer to it in your follow up.
- **a jacket with two pockets.** Put incoming cards in one and outgoing cards in another.
- **a positive, open, and generous attitude.** It is important to remain as positive as possible in these situations.

Lose All Fear of Personal Encounters

When Jack eats out alone, he sits at the bar instead of at a table, because it's much more conducive to striking up a conversation. He even finds that it helps to be friendly with the bartender, because it allows people nearby to see that he is a friendly guy. Here's a recent experience he had:

"I was at a barbecue restaurant and I sat next to a guy at the bar, but I did not end up talking with him, because I missed the opportunity in the first two seconds. I realize now that as I sit down, saying just about anything can be the icebreaker, such as a simple joke about being addicted to good barbecue, or how good it feels to sit down after working 97 hours. It's like sticking a wedge in the door so it won't close, and it sets the stage for a possible conversation. Even just acknowledging the other person and saying 'How ya doin?' as you sit down can open the window for a conversation. But if you sit down in silence and miss that tiny window of opportunity, the whole thing *seems to get 50 times harder, because then you have to break a pre-existing silence with some kind of opening line, and that triggers a whole conversation in my head instead of with this other person in the world.*

"That is not to say that the ice cannot be broken later in a potential encounter, but I think, with some of these mechanisms in place, it just seems much harder. So I try to keep in mind that there is a window that may only last around two seconds. It's very easy to put down a simple placeholder to let the other person know that this could become an encounter; then making it an encounter becomes much easier because that marker was there right from the first moment."

what is small talk?

Most shy people hate small talk—they claim to be horrible at it. But what exactly is small talk? Small talk is the starting point of all relationships. Think of it as a dance you do with someone new to find common ground, a way to ease into a conversation. Through small talk you decide whether "big talk" is appropriate.

When you look around a room and see people chatting, you might assume that small talk comes naturally to most people, but that's not the case. In fact, small talk is not a talent at all, but rather an acquired skill. Small talk is similar to kindling—hopefully, enough branches will burn to ignite the logs of real conversation, which can burn for much longer. Bernardo Carducci says the tag "small talk" connotes that such conversation is trivial and unimportant. On the contrary, small talk is the basis for beginning relationships. It's where we start with almost everyone we meet. So if you can't or won't commit to making small talk, think of all the connections and relationships you'll miss out on.

Technology has truly revolutionized the way people communicate—for better and for worse. David Rose, a Cambridge, Massachusetts expert on computer interfaces, points out that 20 years ago, an office worker had only two types of communication technology: a phone (which required an instant answer) and postal mail (which took days). "Now we have dozens of possibilities between those poles," Rose says. And most of those happen in isolation— e-mail, instant messaging [IM], even the phone. As a result, we are losing both the skill and the desire to make small talk. In today's high-tech society, people are losing the art of day-to-day conversation. It's a skill, if we don't practice it, we will forget how to do it, and we'll resist putting ourselves in situations where that atrophied skill could be of use.

identifying your 10-word blurb

Brenda sometimes finds it hard to answer the simple question, "What do you do?" in a short, concise, and interesting way. Sometimes she rambles on or is afraid she sounds uninteresting. If she gives a pat answer, she fears she'll sound similar to a robot. She wants her "elevator speech" to be perfect, to convey everything there is to know about her in one sentence.

●●●

That's a lot of pressure for one sentence! Many of us get tongue-tied when we have to talk about ourselves or our work, even though so many conversations in our culture start with the question, "What do you do?" It seems simple, but believe it or not, this is often one of the most difficult questions to answer. It becomes even more challenging when what you do is unique, specialized, or new, or when you do a lot of different things.

But first you have to understand the purpose of the question. When someone asks, "What do you do?" his or her goal isn't necessarily to find out what you do. They may want to know, but more than anything, they just want to get a conversation going.

What you say depends on whom you're talking to. Is it a stranger? Someone you haven't seen in a long time but who knows something about you? Someone from a past work experience? Someone from your personal life? If it's a colleague familiar with your industry jargon, using that jargon shows your experience. If it's a new neighbor, your jargon may be intimidating. All of these variables need to be taken into consideration.

Most people won't hear the first thing you say anyway. Remember, there's a lot going on and they will probably only grasp a tiny bit of your interaction, maybe one or two words. But don't worry. It won't be your only chance to answer the question so you don't have to say everything perfectly. Your challenge is to say something that will be easy for them to grasp. To avoid an awkward exchange, it helps to have something ready. That's where your 10-word blurb comes in handy.

Don't answer with a label, unless you are trying to stop the conversation. For example, don't say, "I'm a designer," "I'm a copywriter," or "I'm a lawyer." Although it's short and sweet, it is actually the worst thing you can say. Labels leave too much room for interpretation. They mean different things to different people. If you say you're a "developer" and you mean you're a software developer, but the person you're talking to thinks of a real estate developer, you've already got a miscommunication. Or they may hear your label—"lawyer"—and decide right then and there that they don't need a lawyer, don't like lawyers, or aren't interested in lawyers. Also, the label you use is often industry jargon that you understand, but may not be clear to your listener. For example, few people actually know what a copywriter is or does. Plus, the word "copywriter" is often confused with "copyright," and people may assume a connection to "copyright law."

Instead of labeling yourself, create a blurb that literally says what you do and who you do it for. Here's an example for the copywriter:*"I write direct-mail marketing materials for the healthcare and financial industries."* See how that simple sentence includes what you do and who you do it for? Notice also that it uses verbs and adjectives instead of nouns to paint a picture. Because of that, the listener could pick any of the words in that sentence and say, "Tell me more about that."

creating your 10-word blurb

1.   Your 10-word blurb should answer the question "What do you do?" with three important pieces of information: what you do, who you do it for, and what the end product of your work is. Complete the following formula:

What you do:_____

For whom:_____

What they get:_____

2. Turn that information into your 10-word blurb:

_____

_____

_____.

3. Now write that blurb from a helping perspective:

I help (who?)_____.

create/develop (do what?) _____.

resulting in (so they can...)_____.

4. Now write it from a problem-solving perspective:

I work with (who?) _____.

to solve (problems?) _____.

consequently, (so they can...)_____.

5. Write a version that your mother (or any relative or kindly neighbor you enjoy talking to) would understand. Make it as clear as possible, because this person is genuinely interested but doesn't really understand your business, much less the specifics of what you do.

_____

_____

_____

_____

_____

_____.

6. Write a version that would be understood by a stranger in the doctor's office or your exercise buddy. This is the type of conversation that starts out as chit chat on the topic of whatever brought you together, but could easily turn toward work in those "you never know" type of situations, but only if your blurb is clear. (Also, for all the questions that follow, be sure to imagine yourself talking to people who are positive and who would enjoy helping you, not someone who's going to judge or reject you.)

_____

_____

_____

_____

_____

_____.

7. Write a version that would be understood by a colleague or businessperson you see on a regular basis. This person doesn't know your industry, but does understand business and has connections that could help you.

_____

_____

_____

_____

_____.

8.   Write a version that a colleague at a trade show or conference for your industry would understand. This person understands your jargon, so feel free to use it.

_____

_____

_____

_____.

9.   Try filling in the blanks. One way to be really clear about what you do is the, "You know (blank), well I do (blank)" formula. For example, "You see the sign on top of that building? I make those." What would your version be?

You know: _____?

Well, I do: _____

_____

_____

_____

_____.

10. Describe yourself with a question. Let's say you're an interior designer and someone asks what you do. Your response could be: "Have you ever walked into a room and felt happy just because of the feel of the space around you? That's what I do, I design the interiors of office buildings for creative companies." Or you could be a project manager. Your reply might be: "Have you ever put a meal together for 20 people? You buy all the ingredients, get things in the oven at the right time, and work really hard to have something come out right? Just as you coordinate the meal, I coordinate technology projects, making sure everyone

works together on a new product so it comes out perfect!"
These answers give you a chance to sell yourself because
you're describing how ably you do your work while
describing your work. And don't feel pressured to say
everything. Giving the listener a *memorable* sense of what
you do could be more valuable.

_____

_____

_____

_____.

don't sound like a robot

Now that you've done the preparation and practiced a
bit with these variations on your 10-word blurb, you're ready
to use it. But be careful—there's nothing worse than
sounding as though you're reciting lines you've memorized,
as if you can't remember what you do.

Now that you know what to say, your challenge is to
find a way to say it that is spontaneous, as if it's coming
directly from the present moment and as if it's the first time
you've said it. These techniques will help:

look directly into the person's eyes. That way, even
if you've said it before, this is the first time you're saying it
to this person, and looking at them reminds you of this.

let yourself be imperfect. That's what conversation
is. And if they don't understand, stop and try again.

●●●

" *I don't think you have to be talkative to converse,
or even to have a quick mind. Pauses in conversation
do no harm...What matters is whether you are
willing to think for yourself, and to say what you
think....What matters most is courage. "*
                              —Theodore Zeldin, author
                              *Conversation: How Talk
                              Can Change Our Lives*

be the first one to ask

One of the most challenging situations is introducing
yourself to a stranger about whom you know nothing. How
are you supposed to know what will engage this stranger?
You can't. You can't divine his or her 10-word blurb, and
you can't say, "I'll tell you if you tell me first." The solution:
Ask the question first. This means you have to speak up
first, which is a dilemma for some of us, but one worth
getting over if it means the rest of the conversation will go
more smoothly. If you make a habit of being the first one
to ask the question, you will learn enough to help guide
you toward your best blurb.

conversation starters

Use your blurb to exchange the basics, but don't focus
on yourself. Instead, become interesting, which means
become a good conversationalist. This has two components:
(1) listening well, and (2) bringing ideas, topics, questions,
projects, and your own interesting challenges to discuss. I
am constantly striving to become a good conversationalist,
but some environments are easier than others. There will

no doubt be events or parties where you just don't feel welcomed or in the mood to chat. I recommend that you try to get over that by using your conversation skills and topics.

Here are a few personal examples. Interesting things are constantly happening to me, and probably to you too. Do you take notice of them? You should, if your goal is to become a good conversationalist. All you have to do is notice, remember the anecdote, and then bring it up next time you're in a networking situation.

●●●

I sometimes ride my bike to the train in Hoboken to go into New York City. Recently I got on the train and, without thinking, left my bike helmet on the seat next to me when I got off. I didn't even notice it until a few hours later when I was on my way back to Hoboken. I looked around for someone to ask about the Lost and Found. I noticed a command station at the end of the platform with a big glass window and as I approached, I saw my helmet sitting right there on the ledge, as if it was waiting for me. Someone had obviously returned it. That simple act reaffirmed my faith in people.

Has anything similar to that happened lately? Do you have a feel-good story to share? If so, tell the story and see where it takes the conversation. Here are a few other personal examples that I use as conversation starters:

health issues. Due to osteoarthritis, I'll need a hip replacement sometime soon. I will sometimes bring that into the conversation and ask if my conversation partner knows anyone who's had a hip replacement. I have learned a lot of useful information this way.

current events. You may want to stay away from politics, but you can always talk about the latest scientific discovery, award recipients, sports tournaments, and so on. Movies are generally safe territory and quickly give you a good idea of what kind of person you're talking to.

facts you've learned or books you've read. Bring up a novel, biography, or a business book that you've read, and share a bit of what you've learned. For example, "I've been reading *A User's Guide to the Brain* and I learned that chickens have 25 taste buds, while humans have up to 5,000." Drop that little tidbit into the conversation and see where it goes.

jury duty. I was selected to sit on a grand jury recently and have been bringing it up as a topic in many different environments. Everyone seems to have a story about either avoiding jury duty or enjoying their civic service. What other activity could lots of people relate to?

the food. If there is a buffet, stand near it and make recommendations to anyone who approaches about what's good. Be sure to keep your hands free to shake hands and exchange business cards.

don't just say, "I'm fine"

When someone asks how you are, instead of responding with a bland, "Everything's fine," or "Nothing much." Take the opportunity to highlight a project you're working on. If you've acquired a new skill or accomplished a new goal, mention that. It's not bragging if you focus on the facts.

getting deeper into the conversation

Once you've got your personal introductions out of the way, it's time to dig in deeper. If you take the initiative to lead the conversation, your genuine curiosity could kick in and you'll find yourself asking about something you've heard the other person say. If you don't take the lead, the other person is likely to ask you about something you've said. That's good too and it's one way to convey a good story. Everyone loves a good story, so instead of listing your accomplishments or reciting your resume, tell them a story.

Stories are ideal for a sit-down networking lunch or even on a plane, because they are situations where you can say more than just your blurbs. People tend to relax when they listen, bringing one level of defense down. Also, stories can inspire, motivate, and engage people. We tend to listen closely to stories told with genuine enthusiasm and passion, no matter what the story is about. Your listener may immediately start identifying with characters in your story, thinking to themselves, "Oh yeah, that happened to me too. We have a lot in common." Or, "I need someone to help me with that too."

Tell stories about projects you've worked on, with a focus on the outcome that resulted from the effort you put in— how you were a hero and saved the day! Use examples that your listener will relate to and that reinforce the aspect that would mean the most. Include characters he or she can identify with, a situation that would be familiar, or a crisis that might be similar to the one he or she is in right now. When you're done with a story and there's a pause in the conversation, ask your partner to tell you a story.

follow-up starts while you're talking

Every good networker is also good at follow-up and knows how important it is to reinforce that first impression. But when you sit down to write that follow-up e-mail message or note, unless you've prepared for it, you might think: "I don't know what to say." Here's a little secret to avoid that: Set the foundation for following up while you're talking. This can give you something to focus on during the conversation. As you're talking, look for something to refer to in your follow-up message. As soon as it hits you, make a note of it on the back of the person's business card. Here are a few possibilities:

find something in common. A topic in common—whether personal or professional—is perfect for reaching out later. After the initial follow up, when you come across something related to that topic, you can simply pass it along, and simultaneously remind the other person of your initial meeting.

learn something new. It may be uncomfortable, but lead the conversation in the direction of topics you know nothing about and in which the other person is an expert. Ask lots of questions. For example, if in your questioning, you discover that the person you're speaking to likes horses, or Nascar, or kittens, instead of saying to yourself, "I'm not interested in that," see if you can learn something new. "What the most fascinating thing about horses?" Not only will you learn something new, but in your follow up, you can make a reference to it. And later, when you come across an article or reference to that topic, you can pass it along.

offer an idea, contact, resource. As you're learning about the other person and his or her interests, search your mind for something or someone with whom you can connect. Mention the connection before you part, and then promise to send contact information. When you follow up with, "Here's the information I promised," it shows you're reliable.

Follow up the next day if possible—or, at the very least, before the week is out. If too much time passes before you follow up, the conversation may slip into the recesses of the other person's mind (and yours too) or blur with that of someone else, and it won't have as strong of an impact.

make notes about the people you meet

Exchanging business cards at the beginning of a conversation rather than at the end makes it easier to make notes on the back of the card while you're talking. This will not only flatter the person, it will give you a much better chance of remembering what you talked about, so you can follow up in a more personal way. Written notes also provide the evidence, details, and history you may need to refer to throughout the life of a productive relationship.

Here are a few things to note:

- How will you remember them? Use something they said, something they wore, or a physical trait that stands out.

- What do they need? This will give you something to follow-up about.

- What are they interested in? Just in case you come across something related and need to remember which person mentioned it.

- What notable details about his or her work aren't on the business card? An example would be a specific client or situation he or she mentioned in conversation.

- What commitments should you make to follow up? Did he or she mention never reading e-mail? Then commit to calling, or vice versa.

Writing notes conveys the message that you are detail-oriented, thorough, and that you are going to follow up. If you let them see you doing this, they'll know that you care enough to want to remember.

how to get out of a conversation

Some people have no trouble getting into conversations. It's getting out of them that presents a problem. In reality, you have no obligation to give a reason. When you are ready to move on, you can simply hand over your business card, smile warmly and say, "I've enjoyed chatting with you. I'm going to mingle a bit. Let's stay in touch." But if you need more than that, here a few strategies to try:

get a refill. If there's food or drink involved in the event, say, "I think I need a refill." Or smile mischievously and say, "Excuse me. I need another one of those Swedish meatballs."

involve another person. Find someone to bring into the conversation, then say, "Excuse me while I let you two get to know each other."

stand up. Sometimes you don't have to say anything. Just stand up. Your conversation partner is likely to take the nonverbal cue. He or she may not even be aware of it, but will do the same.

things you can say

- "I've really enjoyed meeting you, but because this is a networking event, I've set myself a goal to meet at least ____ people tonight."

- "I don't want to monopolize you. I'll let you talk to some other folks now. Let's stay in touch."

- "I need to run to the restroom, but let's exchange cards so we can keep in touch."

- "Will you please excuse me? I see someone I need to chat with."

- Also, you can glance at your watch and then say that you need to make a quick phone call to check in with the babysitter, boss, or sick spouse.

eating and schmoozing

The best networking events tend to be the ones that serve some kind of food or refreshment. Those get the most people—at least that's what I have noticed. But eating and schmoozing doesn't always go well together. Eating at an event can be awkward, so choose what you eat carefully. Here are a few ideas to keep in mind:

don't go when you're hungry. Don't approach a networking event that serves food as your ticket for a free meal. Even if the food is plentiful, by focusing on the food instead of the other people, you'll miss opportunities to feed your business the connections it needs to grow. So don't go to an event when you're starving.

choose the least distracting foods. Finger foods are best, especially carrot sticks, chips, and pretzels that won't make your hands dirty. If there is no place to sit down, try to do whatever eating you do without a plate. You'll probably have a drink, which will take up one hand, and if you need a plate, your hands will be unavailable for marketing activities such as shaking hands, handing out business cards, or making notes. If you're talking to someone who is eating, offer to hold his or her plate while he or she gets a business card for you. If you're sitting at a table, you have more freedom to pile up a plate.

keep going back to the buffet. This is actually a strategy for not getting stuck at one table. Don't put more than three bites on your plate. Carry it to a table, introduce yourself to whoever's there, talk (and listen) for 10 minutes, exchange cards, and then excuse yourself to get more food. Repeat until the room is empty.

focus your attention. Don't let your eyes dart around the room looking to see who's arrived, or to look for someone more important or a better prospect. It's easily noticed and makes the other person feel unimportant—which is not a good networking strategy.

watch your drinking and eating. It's easy to overdrink or overeat when you're uncomfortable. Come up with a personal limit before you walk through the door and don't exceed it. That limit could be one drink, or one helping of food, or one dessert. Everyone's limit will be different, and some situations may call for exceptions.

one-on-one meetings

If you're shy and don't like crowds, then one-on-one meetings, interviews, and other types of intimate exchanges may be easier. But sometimes they're not, because if it's just you and another person, there's nowhere to hide. Your first task in any meeting—and especially the first meeting—is to establish rapport. Whether it's a job interview, an informational interview, or a getting-to-know-each-other cup of coffee, be active instead of passive.

go armed with questions. Do your research on the person or the company. Google them and find out what you can about his or her history, what he or she is involved in, if there's anything he or she has written. If the company has a Website, read it thoroughly and refer to what you've read during your conversation. You can even print out a page if you have a question about something. This shows you are serious and well-prepared, which are excellent qualities no matter what the situation.

bring examples of your work. Always bring examples of the work you've done. This will take some of the focus off what you say. If your work is visual, bring a portfolio. But don't hand the portfolio over and watch silently as they flip through the pages. The examples are not as important as how you present them, and the way you use them to build a conversation. Essentially, these are just the props, not the star of the show. Talk through each example or project, but don't be dependent on them. If your work is not visual, bring materials that represent several different projects or jobs you've done. Enhance and elaborate your involvement using storytelling. Describe all you can about what the project was, who was involved, what your role in the process was, what problems came up, and so on.

present your past work with an eye to the future. Samples and past projects are simply a jumping-off point, helping you to make a smooth transition into a conversation about what the interviewer needs and how you may be able to help, whether by providing resources or actually doing some work.

be flexible. Some people will want to spend time admiring your work; others will launch into a speech about themselves, their work, and what they need. Be prepared for either situation and let the other person determine which direction you take. But don't be passive about it; if you're ready to do either, you'll be in a better position to follow his or her lead.

don't ramble. If you're nervous and find yourself rambling on, stop for a moment. Offer a bit of information and then pause to see if there are any questions or comments. Continue the conversation as long as you can.

engage your listeners with stories

One of the reasons you may have trouble talking about your work is because you imagine it will come across as bragging. You should never, ever say, "I'm the best (fill in the blank) on the planet." That, indeed, would be bragging. But you can talk about the work that you do and the effect it has on others, which is not bragging. It's merely stating the facts. First, though, you must make a distinction between yourself and your work. Then just focus on the work. It's a bit of a mind game, but start by avoiding the word "I." Instead, start your sentences with "my clients," or "my projects." Then focus on what you do, and the results it generates. Use verbs rather than adjectives. Leave the adjectives to others in the form of testimonials, or to the press in the form of publicity. Other people can say you're "the best," and it won't sound smarmy at all! One novel way to convey this information is by telling stories about what you do, and what you have done. When someone asks about the work you do, instead of listing your accomplishments or reciting your resume, tell them a story.

4 elements every story must have

1. a passionate voice. Good stories draw people in, and that requires a storyteller who conveys the passion for the business. So add *Evangelist* to your job title, and even if you're the shy type, remember this: Your story is not about you, it's about your work.

2. evidence of your specialty in the industry. You want your prospects to see themselves in the characters in the stories you tell. You'll know when they do because they'll be nodding their heads.

3. a climax. There should be a moment of suspense in your story, and everything should build up to it. If the project you're talking about involved a test, the perfect moment of suspense involves waiting for the results of that test. If the project involved research, the presentation of the data could figure as the moment of suspense. Be creative, and embellish the moment for effect.

4. drama and romance. Romance is not just "boy meets girl." Romance is adventure—romance is life. You can plant little seeds of drama and romance in your story, elements that make people wonder what happened, without giving them all the gory details.

finding your own stories

You don't have to be a writer to tell stories about your work. All you need is a little imagination. Develop four stories that you can use at a moment's notice to engage your listener or reader. Use them in conversation or in writing. Include them in your job interviews, during time with colleagues, or even on a Website in a section called "Success Stories."

tell the story of how you got where you are. Why do you do the work you do?

1. Situation/plot (the problem):_____

_____

_____

_____

_____.

2. Characters (description):_____

_____

_____

_____

_____.

3. Climax (solution):_____

_____

_____

_____

_____.

Story: _____

_____

_____

_____

_____.

tell the story of one of the top three projects you ever worked on. These are also the types of experience you'd care to repeat. Telling this story is promoting the kind of work you want the most and could bring similar projects to you.

1. Situation/plot (the problem):_____

_____

_____

_____.

2. Characters (description):_____

_____

_____

_____.

3. Climax (solution):_____

_____

_____

_____.

Story: _____

_____

_____

_____

_____

_____.

tell the story of a project that wasn't going so well.
An unexpected problem arose, but you took action and
saved the day. This shows the whole picture, acknowledges
the reality of the work you do, and makes listeners trust
you even more.

1. Situation/plot (the problem):_____

   _____

   _____

   _____

   _____.

2. Characters (description):_____

   _____

   _____

   _____

   _____.

3. Climax (solution):_____

   _____

   _____

   _____

   _____.

Story: _____

_____

_____

_____.

tell the story of a project you're currently working on. This will be freshest in your mind and come across with the most details, because it's right on the tip of your tongue.

1. Situation/plot (the problem):_____

_____

_____

_____

_____.

2. Characters (description):_____

_____

_____

_____

_____.

3. Climax (solution):_____

_____

_____

_____

_____.

Story:_____

_____

_____

_____

_____.

2 important questions

These are the two important questions to ask in any job interview.

1. "What is the most important factor in your decision-making process?" If you don't know what's important to the company or the interviewer, you can't make the strongest argument for yourself or your company. This question also helps your interviewer because often he or she needs to ask that very question: With all the different strengths of this candidate, which will be the most important factor to ensure a successful working relationship or project?

2. "If we were to begin working together and we were back in this office a year from now reviewing our success, what will have happened so that you would look back and think to yourself 'This has been an absolutely wonderful investment of my time, energy, and assets?'" In this question, you are asking the other person to imagine working together with a successful outcome, which requires them to establish the parameters of what will define success in the relationship.

always say thank you

No matter what kind of meeting it was, always take the time to thank the other person for the time they spent, whether in person, or on the phone. If you met with several different people, each one should get a customized note of thanks, according to the details of each exchange. Even informational interviews should be followed up with a simple, handwritten note of thanks and the promise to stay in touch.

If it was a job interview, send your note right away, and use it as an opportunity to highlight and/or reinforce your best qualities, which should reflect what you learned when you asked those two important questions. Even if it was clear that the job or project was not a good fit for you, send a note of thanks anyway. Don't abandon the relationship, because you never know where you might meet again.

Hang Up on Phone Fear

There are certain phone calls that Brenda dreads making: calls to upper management about the status of a project (especially if it isn't going well), calls to the media, sometimes even a call to a vendor. She finds herself staring at the phone with a pounding heart and a frozen brain. And even when she writes a script out in advance, she sometimes speaks too fast and forgets to make the most important point.

●●●

There is something about the phone that instills fear in many of us. Even those who have no trouble meeting strangers in person seem to have an abject fear of calling them on the phone. In the words of one very successful writer, "Give me strangers at a trade show any day; just don't make me call them."

One of the prevailing attitudes and excuses for giving in to phone fear is, "If they wanted to talk to me, they would call me." Needless to say, this is not necessarily true.

Plus, it's a passive way to approach business, and life. These are a few other excuses used to explain phone fear:

- You don't want to sound stupid.

- You don't want to bother the other person.

- You don't want to sound similar to a telemarketer.

- You don't think the other person will take your call.

It's true that when we sit face-to-face with another person, we rely heavily on intonation and body language. But when you're on the phone, you are basically blind, because you don't get any of those clues. But if you think about it, approaching strangers in person should be more intimidating than calling them on the phone. You see, on the phone, if the other person is not interested or can't deal with whatever you're calling about at that moment, he or she will likely tell you, and you can both hang up and move on.

when the phone is most appropriate

Some people have a straight preference for the phone; whereas others prefer e-mail. If you know the person you're calling, think first about what means of communication he or she prefers. Next, think about the reason for your call. Some topics need to be handled in a face-to-face meeting. Make sure your decision isn't based on a communication rut. In other words, don't send e-mail because that's what you always do or because that's the way you've communicated historically with this person and it has worked, so why do anything different? The topic may call for something different. That's why it's important to be aware of each situation. Here are four guidelines for times when the phone is most appropriate:

1. when you have something sensitive to say. You want the other person to hear the sound of your voice, and you want to be able to hear the sound of his or her voice when he or she responds. Or if what you have to say could potentially be misinterpreted.

2. when you just need a quick answer. Using the phone indicates urgency in many situations. It conveys the message, "I'm serious about this and would like to take care of it now."

3. when it takes longer to write. Don't waste your time writing when it would be just as easy to pick up the phone and either tell the person or leave a message.

4. when negotiation is required. To find a time or a price, rather than going back and forth endlessly, it often makes sense to simply pick up the phone.

●●●

Conversely, here are three situations when e-mail or a written communication is most appropriate:

1. to confirm a date, time, price, or other specific. If the details could be easily confused, it's useful to have a paper trail and to put in writing what you understood, just in case you didn't have the other person's full attention.

2. when you're contacting someone new. If you aren't familiar with his or her habits or don't know how well he or she processes information, it's useful to use written communication. Again, take a moment to reinforce or repeat what was said, for clarity's sake.

3. to prepare or ask for a real-time conversation. When the issue is complicated and it would be useful to

give the other person a heads up so he or she can be prepared
to talk on the phone or in person.

●●●

Be aware of cultural differences too. For example, the
Japanese consider it impolite to make people speak to a
machine, so they don't use voicemail for business. If you're
still not sure which is the most appropriate medium for
communication, either ask directly, or just follow the other
person's lead. If he or she calls you, call him or her back,
unless he or she specifically says "E-mail is fine." If an e-
mail is sent, e-mail back, unless he or she says, "Call me to
discuss."

be prepared to call

There is nothing better than being prepared to make
phone calls, whether it's one tricky call or several calls of
the same type. Scripts can help you by taking the pressure
off so you don't have to remember what to say. But they
also lock you into a dialogue with very little wiggle room.
You don't want to sound similar to an automaton when
you're in a conversation with someone, especially if it's a
difficult one. To get around this, try writing out your
idealized version of the entire dialogue. This will familiarize
you with the ideas you want to convey and help you find
the most important ones. It will also help you envision a
positive outcome. Then, instead of an actual script, try
working with an outline or a list of talking points. That way,
you can refer to it but it won't leave you speechless in case
the other person doesn't follow the script. Here's what you
need to have ready:

two or three opening statements. These are things that say concisely who you are and why you're calling. Experiment with these opening statements to see which makes the most sense, is more comfortable for you, and which flows with ease. Ask a friend or colleague to listen to you and decide which one to start with. If possible, try them all in the real situation and see what the response is.

two or three questions you want answered. You may not get to all of them, depending on the response. But have them ready, in case the person you're calling is available to chat. Otherwise, leave them in a voicemail message and repeat them in the e-mail follow up.

one or two closing statements. You should include a call to action or next step—what you will do next, or what the other person should do. What do you expect to receive or send to the other person? Follow this up with an e-mail message that reiterates what you've agreed to, especially if it's a difficult situation.

If you have a lot of similar calls to make, do them all at the same time so you can get some momentum going. If you make the calls piecemeal, you'll never get in the groove enough to learn from the experience.

voicemail is your friend

You've done all your preparation, but here's the thing about the phone: More often than not, no matter whom you call, you will get voicemail. So there's really nothing to be afraid of, unless your phone fear is actually "answering machine fear." Have you ever considered the possibility that the person you're calling has phone fear too? That may be why he or she is not answering.

Voicemail rescues everyone from the phone. That means making phone calls—whether you're doing research, trying to coordinate a project, or even cold calling—is more about learning to leave an effective voicemail message. In fact, if you reach a secretary or assistant and he or she offers you a choice between taking down your message and sending you to voicemail, choose the voicemail. You have much more control over what message gets through if you convey it yourself, and there is less chance for your words to be misinterpreted.

Why bother calling if no one ever answers? One simple reason: There is nothing more powerful than your own voice. The sound of your voice—the tone, cadence, softness, formality, where you pause, what you emphasize—it all plays a large part in creating rapport. You can learn how to use your voice to convey who and how you are as a person. Here are a few ideas about how to leave an effective message. If you use a script, practice until you can read it with spontaneity. It shouldn't sound as thogh you're reading from a script. Be conversational and use inflection in your voice. Smile while you read it.

be brief. Don't ramble on. Make sure your script gets right to the point you're trying to make.

start with your headline. Begin with the the core idea, your question, or the goal of your call, and then continue with the details—just in case the other person doesn't listen all the way through.

give your phone number. Always say your contact information at the beginning and at the end of your message.

tell them what you'll do next. And be sure to do it. Let him or her know you'll call again, and that you'll also try to reach them through another medium.

When leaving a voicemail message, the focus of your attention should be on the other person, and specifically what will make it easiest for that person to respond. Sometimes it just requires too much effort. But you can make it easier. Try the one-two punch. E-mail or call, but don't even expect a response to this initial outreach. Plan your strategy to include a second outreach a day or two later. And use the other medium the next time in case the reason for not responding has to do with the medium. And if by chance someone does respond to your first effort, imagine your delight! The problem most people have is that they give up too soon. Getting through to someone, or getting a response, is a result of persistence.

that horribly awkward silence

Once in a blue moon, you'll reach the person you're calling and you must face your fear: that moment of silence on the other end. This is ultimately what everyone's afraid of. It's the moment we hate enough to avoid making calls altogether. But what exactly is so horrible about that "horribly awkward silence"? It's not physically painful or humiliating in and of itself. It is simply a moment of quiet during which you are waiting for what you've said to sink in and for the other person to respond.

The only thing that makes that pause awkward is what you do with it. Start with how you see it. Because in fact, it's not really silence at all. It is simply a pause between words or sentences. Where is your attention during that pause? Is it on yourself? Are you thinking:

● They won't want to talk to me.

- They won't know who I am.
- They won't remember me.
- They won't recognize my name or the name of the referral.

If so, know that you have an alternative. You can take the focus off yourself and direct it toward the recipient of your call. Imagine his or her world the moment you call. He may have calls forwarded to his cell phone and you've caught him somewhere out in the field—in the middle of buying a newspaper or walking down the street. Or he's in the office in the middle of a meeting. Maybe he answered because he was expecting another call, or because he just can't stand missing calls. You have no idea.

With all that going on, your call arrives, out of the blue. All he has is your phone number or company name and what you say about who you are. (Which, if you're nervous and speaking quickly, won't be of much help.)That's why your attention needs to be focused on assessing the situation and reading the other person as quickly as possible—not on what you're going to say. Most of the time there's going to be some silence, so you just have to accept that. But that silence will be as awkward as you decide it will be. Here are four actions you can take to reduce the awkwardness:

1. speak slowly and articulate. Speak clearly when you say who you are and where you're from, especially if you're using a cell phone, which can muffle your voice already.

2. say more, rather than less. Give the other person more to work with. For example, instead of saying "Hi, this is John Smith" and waiting for him or her to recognize you, say, "Hi, this is John Smith from Acme Furniture and I'm responding to the e-mail message you sent me last week."

Somewhere in there, something will click and he or she will know who you are and will be ready to move on to the next stage of the conversation.

3. put the call in context. Remind him or her of the connection between you (if there is one) or the reason he or she might be interested in speaking with you.

4. ask if they have a moment to talk. Don't launch directly into your speech. If you're working with a script, make sure you leave time after you introduce yourself to get a buy-in for the conversation. If he or she doesn't agree to have the conversation, you risk being annoying, and the other person may decide that they don't have time for you.

you can learn in silence

Sometimes, silence is a good thing. The more you can learn to tolerate it, the more you might appreciate the result of it. Because often the other person—who may be as uncomfortable as you are—will fill the silence by saying something unexpected. She may give you information you wouldn't have otherwise thought to ask for, or she may come up with an idea she wouldn't have thought of.

If the idea of creating silence in an uncomfortable business situation makes you more anxious, practice it with colleagues, friends, and family first. You'll be amazed at what you learn.

The skill of reading people on the phone is very important, but becomes impossible to do if you have already decided to dread the call. Those first few moments should be focused on the other person. What you hear and find out will determine the trajectory of the rest of the call, but if you're listening to something inside your head, you'll probably miss it. Here are some of the responses you might encounter and what you could do with each:

if the person is rushed. Acknowledge the time crunch and cut to the chase. Otherwise, your selfishness may annoy your potential customer.

if the person is interested but busy. Ask when would be a better time. Don't confuse this response with a lack of interest.

if the person is uninterested. Don't try to persuade him. Just thank him for his time and hang up.

if the person is open and friendly. This does happen! Use your script and see how it works. Maybe your timing is perfect and you've caught him or her between tasks. Or your timing could be perfect, and he or she was just about to address this issue or look for someone to help on that project.

how to gracefully hang up

Sometimes you're on the receiving end of a phone call that you'd rather not have taken. Yet you still have to end the phone call in a professional and graceful manner. How do you get out of it?

buy time. If the issue being addressed is an emotional one and you are frozen, can't answer, or don't know how to respond, don't panic. Don't give in to the pressure of someone else's emotional state. You can always say, "I need some time to think about that. I'll get back to you."

create a commitment. At the beginning of the conversation, say something similar to, "I've got a meeting in five minutes, but I can talk until then." Then when that time is up, it's not a surprise that you have to move on and say goodbye.

7

Do You Speak Body Language?

Bob and Joe are two creative types who run a small ad agency in New York City. Their target market is the publishing industry, which is not the most conservative industry, but these two always go to meetings wearing suits. It isn't really their style, but they do it because they know that creatives are often stereotyped as flaky, so buttoning up a bit can (and does) help to counter that presumption. Their prospects need them to be reliable and professional, so they go out of their way to convey those qualities in all of their communication, both verbal and nonverbal.

●●●

Perception is everything in business, which is why it's important to project your best image. The quieter you are, the louder your body language. Something as simple as how you sit or stand, or where your eyes land during a conversation with a client or boss, can have a profound effect on how people perceive and respond to you.

113

how your actions may be perceived

Your actions are open to all sorts of interpretation and misinterpretation. If you arrive at an event and sit in the corner, it's probably because you're nervous. But it could be perceived by others as disinterest or arrogance. In a staff meeting, if you close your eyes to think, you may appear bored. Different attitudes are conveyed in different ways. Check whether you are coming across as:

defensive. You might have crossed arms and/or legs, a tightly closed mouth, and clenched jaw. Your eyes could be averted, and you are probably taking small, quick breaths.

embarrassed. You have a nervous laugh, or avoid eye contact, and often turn away, or if you have a flushed face, you might appear embarassed.

nervous or fearful. You are fidgeting, with a lack of focus and nail biting. You are holding your breath, with your eyes darting. You have a rigid or stiff body.

secretive. You keep your distance. Your shoulders are hunched and you have a set jaw. You use a brief, mechanical handshake with downcast eyes.

become aware of your body language

The fact is that most of our body language is beyond our control. Because there are always unconscious forces at work, our body language tends to reveal a lot about our character and emotions—facial expressions, eye blinking, leg crossing, and nervous tapping betray fear, honesty, nervousness, joy, frustration, and so on. Nonetheless, we have more control than we imagine over what people see and the impression we convey. Here are four techniques to use to become aware of what your body is communicating:

1. put yourself in the shoes of the other person. How would you see yourself? In a meeting, or even while waiting on line at the bank, take a moment to step outside of yourself. Choose a person nearby and imagine what that person sees when he or she looks at you.

2. ask a good friend to observe you. Choose someone you trust and ask for an objective perspective based on his or her experience. If you want to know whether you come across as a professional, ask someone familiar with your profession. Tell him or her what image you'd like to convey and ask if that's what comes across. If not, ask what you could do to change that image.

3. listen closely to what others say. Whether in jest or offhand, directly to you or through the grapevine, take what others say with a grain of salt. But don't reject anything simply for emotional reasons.

4. videotape yourself. Simply tape yourself talking about something familiar and listen for how you speak, how you sound, and how often you say "uh" or "like." This is a very objective exercise, and you will likely be surprised by what you see and hear.

take time to prepare

Before a big meeting, most people prepare by worrying—which doesn't help at all. Instead of worrying, why not try strategizing? Take time to think about whom you're meeting with. Are they:

- formal or informal?
- conservative or progressive?
- creative or buttoned-up?
- young or old?

With this information in mind, what impression do you want to convey? This isn't about transforming yourself into someone you're not. Instead the goal is to find out what's appropriate. Your choice should be tailored to the environment you're entering and the type of people you'll be meeting. This decision is, once again, based on the choice between focusing inward on yourself, or outward on others. Focusing outward means thinking about who you will be meeting with—whether at a networking event, a company picnic, or a job interview.

What you hope to achieve in an encounter should dictate how you prepare for it. Think back to your purpose and your goals. For example, if you are a graphic designer attending an event in the financial services industry because you are exploring that market, it wouldn't be appropriate to wear your colorful overalls. You won't fit in and you might alienate the people you are hoping to meet. It would be more appropriate to wear a conservative suit, perhaps with a colorful scarf or tie to hint at your creativity.

It's not so much about what impression you want to convey about who you are deep down, but what impression would be best for that person in that position to receive in order to welcome you and be comfortable talking with you.

the picture of confidence

Keeping in mind that the physical affects the emotional, there are things you can do with your body to convey a message of self-assurance and openness. People will respond to those gestures and actions, which will in turn affect how you feel. The genuinely confident are respectful and position themselves at an appropriate distance for each person they interact with. The confident person:

- walks or strides with erect posture, allowing others to go first.

- has a firm handshake and a self-assured smile.

- makes eye contact and faces the person they're speaking to.

- leans forward when appropriate.

The confident person communicates openness by:

- having a warm, relaxed smile.

- using frequent and prolonged eye contact.

- facing his or her body towards the other person.

- holding his or her arms relaxed with open hands.

- using a firm and prolonged handshake.

controlling your body language

Body language is subject to much interpretation, but less so if you consciously coordinate it with a verbal message. Once you are aware of any expressions you may make, or gestures you have, it will be easier to avoid them. For example, when you approach a speaker at a conference but avert your eyes and turn your body away, what message is conveyed? Certainly a mixed message, and he or she is more likely to hear the nonverbal message more clearly.

Using assertive body language to convey the same message no matter how shy you feel at any given moment, would look like this: You stride confidently toward the speaker with your hand extended, look directly into his or her eyes, and make sure your body is facing him or her directly. Then you make your statement clearly and concisely. When you stop talking, you simply hold still and listen to the response. By being aware of these behaviors and focusing your attention on them as you introduce yourself to a stranger, you can control your body language so it doesn't contradict your verbal message and defeat the purpose of what you are trying to say. The goal is to reinforce your verbal communication with your body language. Good communicators sometimes:

mirror the body language. To make the other person feel comfortable during the conversation, mimic his or her actions. If a colleague leans forward or crosses her arms across her chest while speaking, see what happens if you discreetly mimic her movements.

stride into a room. Do you slump over when you walk? Then make an extra effort to stand up straight and stride into a room. Also, don't rush around. Walk slowly and deliberately, which will also make it easy for others to approach you.

stand at arm's length. You've heard about close-talkers? What about far-talkers? Your tendency may be to keep your distance. Standing too far away suggests that you feel intimidated. Find a middle ground that makes everyone, including yourself, comfortable. A good rule of thumb is to stand about an arm's length from others when talking. Consider personal space and boundaries when communicating face-to-face with another person.

show interest by leaning forward. Leaning forward when listening indicates interest in what the other person has to say.

sit or stand upright. Having your hands on your hips appears domineering. Leaning back in your chair is judgmental. Crossed arms—one of the most common arm positions—often conveys defensiveness or aggression, not openness. Stand up straight and face your audience—whether it's one person or a group. Keep your posture open, with your arms relaxed and hanging at your sides.

stay still. Nervousness often manifests itself as fidgeting, which distracts from what you are saying and reduces the impact of your message. Be aware of each extremity. Avoid hand movements such as tapping or playing with objects, jingling change or keys, scratching or twirling your hair and, of course, biting your nails. Foot shaking is also a clear sign of discomfort.

relax your face. Be careful not to wear your public face in person. You know, the one you use in public places to let people know to keep their distance. Find out if you squint, frown, or make strange faces. Maybe your eyebrows are constantly furrowed? If so, you may come across as angry. Arched eyebrows make you seem surprised or questioning. Frowning can indicate moodiness. Be aware of any artificial, unfriendly, or deadpan expressions you may do subconsciously. The goal isn't necessarily a neutral face. Practice smiling and looking open and welcoming.

make and maintain eye contact. This is one of the hardest things to do if you're shy, but one of the most essential nonverbal skills to master. Averting your eyes can convey many different messages—nervousness, anger, fear, arrogance, or boredom. Or it could mean you're lying. Your goal is to communicate that you are paying attention. Give the person your attention, but don't stare. Don't let yourself be distracted. Don't let your eyes dart around the room or over your shoulder. It's easily noticed and makes the other person feel unimportant. Focus your attention on the person in front of you. If necessary, position yourself so that you won't be distracted by the comings and goings of others. Be attentive to how someone else is receiving your eye contact, and adjust accordingly. You might need to look away from time to time to give the other person a little break.

focus on your voice. Your voice can reveal a great deal about you—more than you want!. People speak quickly when they're nervous. Arrogance comes through in a sarcastic or superior tone. Submissiveness comes across in a soft tone or a whisper. A deep voice conveys authority. This is something you can modulate and control, if you are aware of it. Beyond the tone of your voice, there are many sounds and vocalizations that communicate anxiety, including sighing, coughing, or humming. As a rule, to avoid any mixed messages and help people stay focused on your words and meaning, keep an even and normal voice tone and volume.

breathe evenly. We are rarely aware of our breath, yet it is a clear indication of our stress level, which others may notice. If you're stressed, you may breathe shallowly or even hold your breath, which is accompanied by clenched teeth, a tight jaw, or furrowed eyebrows. Relax and breathe deeply to relax all your muscles.

the power of a strong, confident handshake

You may prefer to avoid touching other people, but when used appropriately, touch can be a very powerful way to convey a message—more than any words you can come up with. The handshake is the most acceptable and the best nonverbal communication we have in business. Studies show that the mere act of shaking hands makes people twice as likely to remember you. What message do you communicate when you shake? Is it a limp shake or a strong shake? Do you offer one finger or the entire hand? Does it depend on whose hand you're shaking? A moment of awareness as you extend your hand can help you shake with confidence, conveying openness, respect, and vitality. A good handshake makes the other person feel welcome.

Make sure your hands are always clean. Always dry your hands thoroughly after washing, and keep food and drinks in your left hand so you won't be caught off guard. If your hands are clammy, keep a handkerchief in your pocket. Offer your hand with the thumb up and fingers together. In your enthusiasm, don't be overzealous. Shaking too hard may come across as aggressive. A limp shake conveys incompetence. If someone offers you a limp hand, temper yours slightly.

A two-handed shake can be a strong statement, depending on whose hand you're shaking. A man using two hands to shake a woman's hand can be perceived as condescending. But a woman shaking another woman's hand this way can be seen as a very warm gesture. Pats and pokes are generally not necessary or appropriate in a business context, but if you want to indicate a bit more warmth or intimacy, touch someone's elbow lightly.

It's also important to know when to stop. Three pumps is plenty, but if the other person won't let go, slow them down by putting your other hand over his or hers, calmly stopping the action. He or she may be unaware of still pumping—perhaps an indication of his or her own nervousness. Remember, chances are you're not the only nervous person! By becoming more aware of your own body language, you can fine tune the way you present yourself to the world.

8

Communication Tools for Introverts

Brenda sees Shirley, a former coworker, in a restaurant. They worked together at another company and haven't kept in touch in the year since. When Shirley walks through the door, Brenda turns the other way in the hopes that Shirley won't see her. Why? There was no bad blood between them; in fact, they enjoyed working together very much. And it's not that Brenda can't remember her name. She just doesn't feel like getting into a conversation.

●●●

Brenda has momentarily forgotten her goals. She's too focused on her own feelings in the moment, and she's not thinking about the unknown possibilities that communication can bring. She's also forgotten that she doesn't know where a conversation will go. It could be good for her to reconnect with Shirley, who happens to know of an open position in her department that would be perfect for Brenda.

Shirley sees Brenda leaving and doesn't have time to follow her, but later that day sends an e-mail to Brenda apologizing for not being able to catch her and telling her about the job. Brenda responds very enthusiastically. This is one time she got lucky and didn't miss out on the opportunity, thanks to Shirley.

●●●

Virtual communication is the perfect medium for anyone who approaches contact with trepidation. Online communication tools, such as e-mail, instant messaging, social networking, and collaborative Websites all make it easy to interact with people at a distance. For the shy and less assertive, these tools have also removed some of the obstacles presented by contact in real time.

But remember: online communication tools are not a substitute for face-to-face contact; there are no shortcuts to genuine human connection. Don't hide behind these tools. If relationships that you develop online are to be strong, they need a lot of effort and attention. Virtual communication is a breeding ground for miscommunication, which also means it requires more attention.

how to avoid miscommunication

E-mail is only one channel of communication, though it's fast and easy. E-mail can document discussions, enable high-impact messages to be sent around the world, and offers a means of documenting a conversation for future reference. But e-mail is also ripe for miscommunication. So be aware of how you're using technology, and ask yourself if you're using the best medium.

For example, when you're in a rush and you respond to a message with a one-liner, your response could easily be misconstrued. Terse e-mails, because they are not accompanied by the writer's facial expression, voice inflection, thoughtful pauses, or body language, can easily come across in the wrong way.

We don't realize how much we rely on nonverbal and visual communication until it is absent. If there is any doubt as to how a message will be received, take pains to prevent a potential miscommunication by waiting five minutes before clicking send. If you're angry when you write the message, take this exercise one step further. Get up and walk around, or do something else, before you write the message.

how to approach someone online

Finding and developing relationships online in the business world is here to stay. But if you want to communicate, first you need to get someone's attention—and that is often a challenge. Instead of undivided attention, sometimes the best we can achieve is something called "continuous partial attention," in which we are so busy keeping tabs on everything else that we never focus on any single item or person. Is the person you're trying to reach simultaneously juggling new messages, documents, spreadsheets, and browser windows? Whether it's someone you know (a colleague or client), someone who knows you (your boss or a vendor), or even a stranger (a prospect or friend of a friend), your goal is to find a way to break into his or her space, cut through the clutter and get his or her attention.

●●●

The window through which the other person can take in your communication is small, whether it's an e-mail message, an instant message, or even a voicemail. You have to make sure your message is small enough to fit through that window. If it does, and he or she receives it at a moment when he or she can focus on it, you might get a response. You volley it back by saying just a little more, building on the initial communication, or adding a few details or examples. But often what happens is that we give up when we don't hear back right away, and don't try again. Unfortunately, if you don't remain insistent, you'll never get to the dialogue stage.

writing e-mail that actually gets read

As our attention spans shorten, the prevalence of e-mail rises. If you want your recipients to read and respond, you need to write short, concise e-mail messages that ask directly for a response. If they move on to the next message without answering yours, there is less chance of them getting back to your e-mail. Think about the person you're writing to. How does the message need to be presented in order to be grasped quickly? What will make the most sense? What will be familiar or interesting enough to make him or her stop and read it? The main rule is to keep it short and simple. Long e-mail messages are the online equivalent of rambling in a conversation. In the virtual world, no one has the time or attention for that. And while long sales letters are often successful in direct response marketing, it's not usually appropriate for one-on-one communication. So unless someone is expecting a long message from you or has asked a question that requires a lengthy response, don't do it. Here are a few guidelines to make sure your messages get a response:

make your subject line clear. Ideally, your subject line should be a one-line summary of your message or topic. If the goal of your message is to get an answer to an important question, make the question your subject line. And if you are reusing a message from an old thread, change the subject line to reflect the current topic. Otherwise you may confuse the recipient.

remind the recipient of who you are. If you're writing to a stranger or someone with whom you don't have regular contact, remind him or her of who you are and how you are both connected.

be direct. Make your expectations clear at the top of the message. Ask a question or state your need up front. Don't make the recipient search for it.

ask for a response. If you want a response, state at the beginning what you have to offer, what it's going to do for him or her, what you need, and what to do.

be clear about action items and priorities. Spell them out, either as lists or bulleted items. This will help the other person prioritize the most important information.

put pertinent information and links at the right place and time. For example, if you write, "Call me," put your phone number next to those words so the other person doesn't have to search for it.

don't end with "hope to speak to you soon." "Please get back to me" is the worst way to end an e-mail. Tell the person what you want him or her to do and what you'll do next.

call out your expectations of each person. Especially if you're writing to multiple recipients! This way, the recipients will not have to wonder what another person is working on.

don't give all the details. Summarize in bullet format, then make it easy for the recipient to call you to initiate a conversation to discuss the details.

don't address too many issues at once, or ask several questions in a single message. Instead, send one question per message. Or if you know the person won't appreciate a bunch of messages, open your message with a summary of the various issues and indicate which are the priorities.

indicate if no response is necessary. Put "No Reply Necessary" at the top. This will help the other person prioritize incoming information.

don't delete the original message. When replying to a message, especially if more than a few hours has passed, don't assume the other person will remember what it was about, or what you said. You should always include the prior e-mails below your current message.

don't send too many attachments. If you have more than two documents to attach, consider combining them into one document. And be sure to indicate in the body of the message what documents are attached, and what format they are in.

don't leave the body of the message blank. Always indicate what you are attaching. It's not always obvious to see. And if something can be conveyed in the body of the message, do so rather than include an attachment.

don't abuse e-mail addresses. Unless you have permission, don't add someone to your e-mail list, whether it's for social, business, marketing, or private jokes.

don't pass along anything that could be a hoax. Do your research online to determine whether a chain e-mail is valid, or if it's just a hoax or rumor. Usually just typing a few key phrases into Google will relay the truth.

don't make a group of addresses public. Unless the people are all part of a group and will want to reply to all to communicate about a specific issue, create an address list that keeps the address and names of the recipients hidden.

always include your signature file. Your signature should contain your contact information, especially your phone number and e-mail address. This way the other person can reach you quickly, without having to hunt for your information.

always check grammar, spelling, and punctuation. Avoid typos and mangled sentences. It's not rational, but often people make personality judgments based on grammar and spelling, especially when that's all they have to go on! Make sure you leave a positive impression.

continue to use a greeting until your recipient stops doing so. Even if you're going back and forth with someone and it doesn't seem worth the time to keep using his or her name in the salutation and signing off with yours, do it anyway. Take the lead from a customer or supervisor and let him or her become informal first.

check who your message is being sent to. There are lots of horror stories about e-mail messages being sent to the wrong recipient. Look to see whose address actually comes up when you're typing, and look before you click send.

be aware of who is copied on a message. Reply only to the original writer instead of replying to all the recipients.

send large files in a zip format. If you are sending large files as attachments, be sure to zip the files before you send them. This minimizes the space, and will help the other person keep his or her inbox neat and organized.

e-mail tips for shy managers

Virtual communication isn't just for people who work remotely. Many people are finding it easier to send an e-mail or instant message to someone on the other side of the office than get up and talk to them. As a manager of a team, you may also be tempted to use e-mail to manage your team, whether they are far-flung or all in one place. E-mail should certainly have a role in your communications, but beware of trying to manage groups of people through e-mail. Your presence won't have impact, you might not reach everybody, and it's more difficult to assess whether they actually read your message. Here are four ideas for the best ways to deal with your team via e-mail:

1. let your team know when they can expect a response. Schedule your e-mail time and be as consistent as possible. If you can't keep up, delegate some of the responsibility.

2. encourage people to reply with their questions. This is similar to having an open-door policy.

3. use smiley faces strategically. A smiley face can clarify if there's a doubt or ambiguity in your message. But too many will erode the meaning of your message.

4. don't hide behind e-mail. Save your criticism, corrections, and anything likely to inspire emotion for face-to-face meetings. You will control your message and the emotions of your team member much better by delivering the bad news in person.

when you shouldn't use e-mail

One of the dangers of these virtual tools is that we get into a rhythm that sometimes becomes a rut. It's essential to know when to go from virtual to real-time communication. Here are four situations when it's better to pick up the phone:

1. at the last minute. If you're canceling plans or can't show up to a meeting, don't convey that message with e-mail. If there's any question about whether your changes will be received in time, call instead.

2. when it's urgent. You never know if and when e-mail is received, so if you have an urgent question or piece of information to deliver, do it in real time.

3. when it's about money. As soon as someone asks for specifics similar to pricing and timing on a project—something that can be negotiated—it's time to talk. To jump into real time, simply write, "Let's have a short chat to discuss your needs and I'll be in a better position to give you prices." Then suggest a time to talk.

4. when the issues are quite complex. Virtual communication is best for simple back and forth, such as making and confirming appointments, or providing details that would be a challenge to remember. If the issue requires some thought and it would take longer to write something clearly, pick up the phone.

when to use instant messaging (IM)

Instant messaging—it's turbocharged e-mail. Many business people prefer the immediacy and streamlined efficiency of IM to that of phone calls and e-mail. In its report, "IM: The Sleeping Giant," the technology consultant Gartner Group predicted that instant messaging will soon surpass e-mail as the primary online communication tool. But e-mail is still king, and more than half of the instant messaging being done is personal. Peggy Duncan, productivity expert and author of *Conquer E-mail Overload*, thinks too many people spend too much time on e-mail. "It's just another barrage of interruptions. It's faster for certain things, but it shouldn't be substituted for the phone because it can take twice as much time."

what IM is good for

Instant messaging enhances collaboration, so it is ideal for groups and teams that work together on projects. It's also well-suited to providing quick information about project status, meeting times, or a person's whereabouts. And it's perfect for answering quick questions in a customer-service environment, doing quick research, and getting fast information. According to Peggy Duncan, it does not lend itself to developing new relationships, or for dealing with complicated issues.

how to use IM effectively

IM saves time, because you can dispense with some of the pleasantries. "Hi, do you have a second?" is sufficient when you reach out to someone via IM. But asking for permission is crucial, as you would (and should) when calling on the phone. Once you have permission, proceed with your question, but get to the point right away. Keep your instant messages simple and brief. Also, to use IM effectively, you must be disciplined about how and when to use it. Turn it off when you don't want to be interrupted. Know when to say goodbye. "Back to work" will do it.

the dangers of IM

Much has been written about the way IM threatens the workplace. Because it's more informal, and is populated by fragments, one liners, one word sentences, and emoticons, it's easy to let your guard down. But don't forget that these exchanges are usually archived, which may be embarrassing later. Anyone can simply copy and paste the entire chat onto a notepad or Word document. Don't use IM to:

- chastise a boss, employee, or coworker
- reach out to those who haven't invited you to do so
- say anything that you wouldn't say in public
- communicate confidential or sensitive information

using those new social-networking tools

In his best-seller, *The Tipping Point*, Malcolm Gladwell quotes sociologist Mark Granovetter on the strength of weak ties: "When it comes to finding out about new jobs—or, for that matter, gaining new information, or looking for new ideas—weak ties tend to be more important than strong ties. The most important people in your life are, in certain critical realms, the people who aren't closest to you, and the more people you know who aren't close to you the stronger your position becomes."

This theory has also come to be known as "six degrees of separation," and social networking Websites and online communities such as MySpace, LinkedIn, Friendster, and Orkut have been created to help their members benefit from the idea. Writes Krista Bradford in the Wall Street Journal, "These sites have programmed into their source code the algorithmic expression of six degrees of separation. They have the technology to show that you know someone, who knows someone, who knows someone you *really* want to know."

These Websites try to help people use those connections by mapping them out and giving members a way to get in touch with others. Once you join, you can upload your contact database, which is then cross-indexed with every user's contact database to reveal connections. You simply look up someone you want to meet and chances are you can get an introduction through your friends.

For those reluctant to network in real time, these sites provide a good networking option. Some people use the sites to find a job, business partner, or an apartment, or to track down a former colleague. More human resource executives and recruiters frequent these sites—making them perfect places to network for a job. (They're especially popular in information technology, because IT professionals are usually comfortable with the latest technology.)

●●●

Social-networking sites allow you to write a profile describing your work experience, key specialties, and career history. The profile serves as a sort of resume, without actually advertising that you're in the market for a job. If you want that fact made public, some sites let you do so.

When asked what kind of networking you're interested in, you simply check the box for "to find a job." However, recruiters worth their salt will approach you if your credentials are impressive and in demand, even if you don't check the box. Of course, the value of social- and business-networking sites isn't limited to job hunting. You can leverage contacts made on the sites for business deals, or to secure venture capital and consulting assignments. You can even research the competition and track products in the marketplace.

It isn't enough to just become a member of one of these sites. You have to actively maintain your personal profile, invite others to join your network, and use the site to search. Most of the rules of successful face-to-face networking also carry over to online networking. It's about a long-term strategy rather than the quick fix. Use these networks to create visibility and to help others in a way that results in trusting relationships.

do your research. Social-networking sites make it easier to learn about your colleagues and prospects and to make educated guesses about what you can do for them. You can learn things about colleagues that you wouldn't otherwise know. Peering into their address book gives you insight into their world. You can get a better sense of the other person or company both personally and professionally. This kind of knowledge is quite powerful if you use it wisely.

do for others. Just as in off-line networking, the more you do for others, the more they'll want to do for you, and the stronger your relationship will become. That means your own requests will seem less like impositions later on.

join more than one. Although some overlap exists, each social networking site offers opportunities to network with different sets of people.

don't endorse. Some of these sites allow you to endorse other people, but keep in mind that the endorsement always reflects on you. Be cautious and only praise someone who's truly exceptional. It gets even trickier if a client or a boss asks you for an endorsement. How do you decline without offending him or her? There's no easy answer, although some sites help with those requests by providing several choices: accept the request, reject it, reject the request and say why, or not respond. If you aren't comfortable endorsing or linking to someone, simply say, "I don't know you well enough at this point." That is a softer way of saying it, and it leaves the possibility for a future endorsement open.

be selective. Don't answer every message. Once you get involved, you may be asked to pass on requests from other members to your prominent contacts. Be selective about what you choose to relay, or you may damage your standing with your influential friends.

using blogs, e-mail lists, and online bulletin boards

There are so many places you can go online to join in a discussion. Sometimes the discussion will even come to you, as it does when you sign up for e-mail discussion groups, also known as a listservs. There are e-mail discussion lists devoted to just about every topic imaginable, both personal and professional. Members post messages asking for or offering advice. The messages are sent to the group on a daily, weekly, or monthly basis. Internet newsgroups are also valuable as virtual networking tools. You can find them through a variety of resources, including Google Groups, Yahoo! Groups, and Topica. Web forums or bulletin boards

are only slightly different, in that they are specialized Websites and they are sometimes mo a host. Participants post messages in response t and members can read and reply at any time. V are similar to group conversations.

are only slightly different, in that they are hosted at specialized Websites and they are sometimes moderated by a host. Participants post messages in response to questions and members can read and reply at any time. Web forums are similar to group conversations.

Selling Techniques for Shy Salespeople

As a business-unit manager for a professional-services firm, Richard was responsible for both sales and delivery. Some members of his team, more often designers than software developers or business strategists, hated going on sales calls. Some of them actually begged him not to make them sell. After probing around, he discovered that the source of their fear came back to objections. "I tried talking to people on a rational level, explaining that they were the expert and that they were fully prepared to manage objections. But it didn't fully work. They simply did not want to be put on the spot. They found defending their process demeaning and degrading."

●●●

You may find yourself in a position where you have no choice but to be a salesperson, whether you're selling your own or someone else's talents, services, or products. Perhaps you were promoted into the position that gives you more visibility and responsibility for a new business or moved from management to sales to avoid a layoff. Or maybe you started your own business because you love the work and want nothing more than to do it. Little did you know you'd have to learn how to sell it, too!

Either way, you don't like the image of the slimy salesperson and are afraid that if you sell, that's how you'll come across. Well, go ahead and breathe a sigh of relief right now because the stereotypical image of the salesperson is not the only one there is. It's not even the most effective one. Take a look at this list of the qualities of excellent salespeople. They are:

- good listeners
- skilled at reading people well
- excellent at building relationships
- detail-oriented
- good at one-on-one relationships

what is selling?

If marketing is every little thing you do to get the word out about your company, then selling is everything you do once they're there. Selling includes providing information about the product or service in the form and structure the customer needs to receive it, and answering specific questions the customer has and moving them closer and closer to the close—that is, the moment he or she says yes or hands over the credit card or check. This moment should actually be called "the opening," because it is the beginning of a relationship, not the end! Whether it's yourself or your talents, your company's products or services, here's what it takes to sell:

a positive attitude. First and foremost, you must truly believe that your efforts will pay off. If you approach the selling process negatively, you will engage in a self-fulfilling prophecy. If you try to sell reluctantly, it will take even longer. You must adopt a can-do attitude—a "Let's try to figure this out" approach—even if you don't feel can-do, especially at the beginning, when all is unknown.

distance and objectivity. In order to sell anything, you have to step away, see it as something separate from yourself, and take nothing personally. You may be excited when someone buys what you're selling, but as much as possible, resist the urge to be either excited or depressed about the results. If you see the process as impersonal, you will be less attached to the outcome. It will be just like anything else you do.

passion. This may seem to be a contradiction, so read closely. You must be passionate about what you're selling. If you're doing something you love, you'll have the enthusiasm because you love your work. If it's your business but it's not built on a passion, you'll need to find that passion somewhere. It could even be in the process. Be passionate about the work and dispassionate about whether or not people buy. The more passionate you are, the more the customer will want to buy.

enthusiasm. Your enthusiasm for selling must be real and it must come through, even if you're afraid of letting it show. Enthusiasm is contagious and lubricates the selling process. Your buyer will probably catch your enthusiasm, which will make the selling process that much easier for you and your company or business.

persistence. You must have a dogged unwillingness to take no for an answer. It takes at least seven contacts before a prospect becomes a customer. That's seven calls or letters or meetings that end with maybe. So you can't be someone who gives up easily. This is where distance and objectivity comes in handy. If you can see that it's not you who is being ignored or rejected, it will be much easier to keep calling, keep pushing, keep following up, and that's what's necessary for you to become a truly successful salesperson.

realistic expectations. You may want selling to be easy. You may want your customers to buy from you right off the bat, which may happen from time to time. But it's not the norm, so adjust your expectations to fit reality, or else you will become discouraged very early in the process and those feelings will threaten to determine your actions. Remember your goals and let them guide you. Don't become distracted by your feelings, which are not always related to reality.

a strategy to follow. Without a strategy or plan to follow, you are unlikely to close your best prospects. It's up to you to lead them through your sales process. Here's a basic sample strategy. You're selling documentation services for software developers. You do the initial prospecting through telemarketing to generate qualified leads (those in the best position to utilize your product or services) that fit the criteria of your ideal customers. Out of that effort, you get a list of qualified prospects who have expressed an interest in your services. Now what?

How are you going to reach out to these people again and again until they're ready to buy? Each customer is in a different position with different needs and a different time frame. You need a structure that can be applied to everyone, but also something that can be tailored to fit the specific needs of each lead. Will the customer want to visit your Website before you making a commitment to invest any time? Will he or she want to receive written materials to review and show to colleagues before meeting with you in real time? Will he or she want to have a phone conversation first to find out what you offer? This is one more situation where reading people and determining their needs is essential. Otherwise, you could botch the selling process.

The major marketing materials you need to take qualified prospects through a selling process include:

- a brochure or other written materials to send
- a Website
- a phone script
- an e-mail newsletter or other method to reach out with valuable information
- contact management software
- a sales presentation

Your prospects should hear from you on a monthly basis if they are qualified leads. You need a calendar that schedules what they'll receive from you each month, such as a mailing, a phone call, an e-mail newsletter, and so on.

> *Cold calling for me has not always been easy. I've been in the Sales and Marketing game for 30 years, but overcame my fear by being curious. The call is easy to do when I get curious about the prospect or customer. I'm curious about what they think, why they use what they use, and who they are. When I shift the focus on them and not on me, the fear goes away."*
>
> —John Charles

the cold call

We sometimes freeze up during cold calls, for fear of being judged and rejected. Perhaps the lack of face-to-face contact is frustrating because it's harder to establish a relationship without eye contact and the cues relayed through body language. You may know your pitch quite well, but if it's expressed without conviction, it's less likely to succeed. Every call gets harder, with self-perpetuating cycles of vulnerability and defeat.

To thaw your fear out, spend more time establishing a connection with the person you're calling before launching into your pitch. And train yourself to tune in to verbal cues. These cues can give you the extra information you need to clinch the sale.

the sales presentation

Most prospects won't take the time to meet with you unless they are serious about working with you or buying from you. There's just no time for "getting to know you" meetings unless there's a need in clear sight. When your prospect is ready, your job in an initial sales presentation is to both provide the details about what you're offering, and to find out as much as you can about your prospect's needs. This is not an interrogation. Your career is not on the line, even though it may feel that way. Keep it all in perspective and acknowledge your own personal power in each situation. You and your prospect are interviewing each other to establish fit and compatibility. You'll be much more relaxed if you think of the meeting in this way.

Preparation is also a key to success. Be sure to have materials ready to show, whether you're giving a standard PowerPoint presentation or handing out supplemental information. Either way, find the balance between presenting the information you've prepared and following the prospect's lead into other areas, even if it feels as though you're going off on a tangent. This tangent may be unfamiliar, but it will probably relate more directly to your prospect's needs. Know your stuff well-enough to move in any direction. If all your efforts are focused on getting back to your script, the conversation will be disjointed.

responding to objections

Wouldn't it be great if you gave your sales presentation, the prospect posed questions you knew all the answers to, and at the end of the conversation, your prospect simply asked "Where do I sign?" This happens from time to time, but it's nowhere near the norm. In fact, beware of people who act too quickly or make decisions impulsively, especially if you're selling a big ticket item. You will develop trust by suggesting they take some time to consider the purchase, to see if any more questions come up. It's true that you risk losing the business by doing this. The customer may have second thoughts, or even come across a better option, but you will be better off in the long run. Experience shows that the relationships that go sour are often the ones entered into impulsively and without due consideration.

The norm is to deal with someone who's interested but unsure, and who probably has questions about your product or service. It's your job to set him or her straight and clarify these points. Some people call these objections. Those same people call this process "overcoming objections," but that language implies a power struggle, and that's not what selling should be.

When your prospect questions you about your product or service, he or she wants to find out more. Although it may be uncomfortable, and the tone of the exchange may sound aggressive to your ear, keep in mind that you may not be hearing or reading her accurately. The other persons tone may have nothing to do with you. He or she may be defending against his or her own images of stereotypical salespeople. Don't be fooled—there is no confrontation here. Think of it as a conversation or a dialogue with questions and answers. You job is to answer the questions. Acknowledge that you understand the concerns and questions. Don't assume that the question are the same as those of other prospects. Listen closely, letting him or her know you have understood what he or she is saying. Even if you are sure you have understood correctly, this helps to demonstrate that you aren't jumping to conclusions.

One tool that will help both you and your prospect is a list of frequently asked questions or concerns. That will prevent you from feeling "on the spot" and your mind from going blank. Even if you momentarily forget the answer to one of these questions, you can simply refer to the FAQ and read it aloud to your prospect. If your prospect asks a question that is not yet on your FAQ, and you don't know the answer, don't feel pressured to answer. Give your best response and, if it's incomplete or unclear for some reason, tell him you will do a little research and get back to him about it. Then be sure to do so right away.

prepare your responses to common objections

No matter what type of business you're in, there are a few statements that prospects use when they want to stall, or aren't convinced you're the right person for them. You won't always be able to work past this stage in the process, but if you back off without responding, you'll miss out on those opportunities you could win. Again, preparation is key. Be ready with a few ways to respond to these common objections:

you're too expensive/we can't afford your prices. The customer may not be aware of how your pricing works. Offer alternatives for him or her to consider. If you really want this customer and are willing to offer a freebie to get your foot in the door, this is the time to make the offer.

we don't have the budget. This is different from "You're too expensive," and reflects an opening that you shouldn't let slip by. Ask what they mean. No budget at all for this type of work? No budget left for this year? If the latter, find out when the new budget kicks in, or when budget planning will resume, so you can get back in touch then.

we already have a supplier. Yes, but is he or she happy with the current supplier? This is the perfect time to ask. Find out what the other persons likes and doesn't like about the current supplier. That will give you essential information about which of your benefits to emphasize, either now or later, as you continue the marketing process. Your prospect may be staying with his or her current supplier because it's too much effort to find someone else.

Your job in this case is to reinforce all the reasons why working with you or buying your product would make life easier. You might have to convey this message bit by bit over time, but don't neglect to use this information if you can get it. Also, the customer may need a back-up resource at the drop of a hat, and if you're waiting in the wings, you'll be well-positioned to fill the need.

we're not in the market for that right now. This is the best objection to hear, because it means the issue is timing. All you need to find out is when he or she may be in the market again. Then be sure to reach out before that window of time arrives. The process of selling will be much easier when you've made a second contact, as the customer will be familiar with you and your product.

how to ask for the sale

You've come this far. You've identified the need, provided ample material, and demonstrated that you have the expertise and/or the product to satisfy the need. You've answered all the questions, overcome the objections, and now there's only one more thing to do: Ask for the sale. And yet this is precisely where many of us fall down. We don't follow through. We tell ourselves, "If he or she wanted it, he or she would let me know." And that may be true for some, but it's dangerous (and a huge waste of your time up to this point) to make that assumption. You must ask for the business. You must "close the sale," as many sales trainers call it.

Thomas Murphy, author of *Selling for Introverts*, doesn't agree with that terminology. His chapter on this topic is called "Asking for a Commitment" and in it he writes: "Asking for a commitment implies an understanding of the sales message and an agreement that the product or service is indeed a solution to the buyer's problem or a positive contribution to that person's personal or business life. It isn't a 'close;' it is an opening of a relationship with responsibilities and expectations. 'Close' would be more appropriate when a sale is not made." Murphy goes on to provide five sure signs that your prospect is ready to buy. Here's what you should watch for:

- The prospect asks about payment terms.

- The prospect asks about timing and when you could get started.

- The prospect speaks negatively about a current supplier.

- The prospect provides proprietary information.

- The prospect wants to meet the other people in your organization or company that he or she would be working with.

When you see or hear one or more of these signals, you can relax and move confidently toward the commitment. Now it's just a matter of working out the details. Still, there is one caveat (and a cliché): Don't count your chickens before they're hatched. Manage your expectations and know that the deal is not sealed until the contract is signed and money has changed hands. Don't pressure anyone to buy before they're ready, but find the balance between getting them ready and moving the process along so it doesn't drag on longer than necessary. Here are a few ways to ask for the commitment:

outline the next step. "Have I answered all your questions? If so, and you're ready to make a decision, here's the next step in the process." Then you tell the customer there's a contract to sign, a meeting to schedule, or all that he or she has to do is provide a credit card number. Don't ever leave it up in the air as to whether the customer has made the commitment. Ask the other person directly, "Are you ready to sign the contract?" or "Are you ready to set up the first working meeting?"

make it easy. Do everything you can to make it easy for your prospect to take that next step. There should be an activity he or she does to make the leap from prospect to customer, such as a sign a contract, fill out a questionnaire, or pay an invoice—something to make the process official. This also helps engender trust and professionalism. Volunteer to send this document, rather than waiting for the other person to ask for it.

give a deadline. People often need to be nudged before they take action. There has to be a sense of urgency, and you can create that. Put a deadline on the sales process. "We have one slot left for this month" or, "This is one of our last few products before the next shipment." The sense of urgency often tips the scales in your direction. If it doesn't work on this prospect, that also tells you there may be something else holding up the process and you need to find out what it is. You may have a bit more selling to do.

offer an incentive. If he or she is still hesitating and you're sure all questions have been answered, try using an incentive. Offer a discount with a deadline, or a freebie if he or she signs on before a specific date.

10

Managing Shy People

Andy has an interview for a new job. He's perfect for it, has all the right skills and talents. He's sure he could do the job well if he could just get past the interview. But he's afraid he won't find the right words to answer the questions coherently, that he'll forget his most recent success story, and that he'll stammer, hesitate, turn red, maybe even forget his own name. If he's lucky, his interviewer will be aware of this discomfort and try to help him through it.

●●●

As a manager, you are bound to have a shy or quiet person on your team at any given time, and he or she may require a little extra attention. Not because they're problematic, but because he or she needs some help and a little coaxing to come forward with new ideas. Just because someone is quiet doesn't necessarily mean he or she is uncommunicative or unsure of themselves. It just may take a little longer for them to open up. Your goal is not to fix the shyness or to make him or her less shy. Shyness doesn't necessarily need fixing, although sometimes people want to grow out of it, and you can be in a position to help.

Shy people often have a limited comfort zone, and you can help expand their comfort zone as it relates to their performance at work. You can do that systematically. Don't address the issue of shyness on the basis of personality. Instead, handle it on a functional basis. If there's something that needs to be done and your employee's reluctance is getting in the way, focus on the task that needs doing rather than the larger issues related to personality.

●●●

Colleen Cannon, who managed dozens of people during her 25-year career with a Midwest publishing company, says shy people are often the least demanding employees to supervise because they rarely seek out attention from you as a manager. But because the shy ones prefer to stay below the radar, you may not be getting all they have to offer. "It's important for you to meet often with the quieter members of your team," advises Cannon. "Encourage them to share their ideas regularly and to speak up if there's a problem. Most of all, don't let *their* discomfort about communicating get in the way of you setting clear objectives and giving specific feedback about their performance."

helping shy people contribute or participate

Most of the time, shy people select projects and positions that suit their personality and don't put them in the limelight. But sometimes, they do such a good job that they are promoted into a position with more responsibility and more visibility, requiring them to speak up and present to groups.

With sensitivity from you, your shy employee can blossom. Bernardo Carducci, director of the Shyness Research Institute at Indiana University–Southeast, advises managers to encourage shy employees to speak up in meetings, and give them extra time to do so. Expand their comfort zone systematically. If they can't do it right away in a business context, offer the opportunity to practice speaking up around people with whom they feel comfortable. If you're conducting a meeting, "Never ask them to go first. Don't expect a rapid response, and don't move on too quickly or talk over them," says Carducci. "Tell them that everyone will contribute so they can prepare ahead of time. Then give everyone a chance to respond." Here are four ideas to make your shy employees feel more comfortable:

1. listen more. Sit quietly and let the other person express himself at his own pace. Adjust to your employee instead of trying to get him to work or speak at your pace.

2. allow time for preparation. If you know an employee doesn't respond well on the spot, provide time and materials, such as a meeting agenda, so she can prepare in advance.

3. understand. What is your employee's preferred communication style? Speak to him in his most preferred style, not your own. A shy person may feel more comfortable writing an opinion on a topic, so experiment with different communication tools, rather than requiring everyone to do the same thing.

4. confirm and reflect. You can repeat back to her that you understand what she is saying. "So what you are telling me is...." This will help not only to make sure that you do in fact understand, but will also give her a feeling of support and trust.

In a team environment, such as a brainstorming session, you may have to work harder to make sure you're not passing over the quiet ones. One very effective strategy used by Sheila Campbell, president of Wild Blue Yonder, a consulting firm that focuses mostly on creativity thinking, involves a combination of silence and Post-it notes.

"You get fabulous ideas from the shy people," says Campbell, "but they won't fight their way into the conversation. They need quiet time to sort their thoughts out. So in the retreats we lead, we give everyone a pad of Post-its and let them write their ideas, anonymously if they want. Then we collect all the Post-its to prevent any censoring. That way, we get all the ideas and all the different thinking styles. Also, the ones who need time get to think and write before they speak. That way, if they are called on, they have notes and are prepared, so they feel more competent. Also, this controls the extroverts, who sometimes get out of hand."

Campbell also advises against going around a circle and forcing people to give ideas in order. "That's the worst thing you can do to a shy person. It doesn't foster any creativity. Most participants, and not just the shy ones, will be busy dreading their turn rather than thinking up a great idea."

If your employee does want help overcoming shyness, there are many ways to help: Provide training when they want it, such as Toastmasters, where he or she can learn basic presentation skills in a safe environment. Or you can encourage him or her to make a videotape while talking, and watch it together. This allows you to see things that you wouldn't otherwise see, such as unnecessary gestures.

how to give an artful critique

Offering feedback and criticism is one the most important tasks of a manager. But how best to offer feedback to a shy person without it being taken as "criticism" or a personal attack?

Because giving feedback is rarely all good news, it's best to find out first if the timing is right for your employee to hear or receive the feedback you have. Shy people can't always say, "This is not a good time for me." So approach with, "I'd like to tell you something, is now a good time? Are you prepared to discuss this?" Your question offers the opportunity to prepare and think about the issue, which he or she may not ask for independently.

Then, when giving your feedback, the focus must be on what has been done and what needs to be done, rather than on the person's personality. In his 1995 best-seller, *Emotional Intelligence*, Daniel Goleman offers guidelines for "the artful critique" (paraphrased and adapted from Harry Levinson, a psychoanalyst turned corporate consultant):

set aside time. Don't wait for an annual review if something needs to be addressed. Make the time to address the issue in person with your employee, preferably in a relaxed and stress-free environment.

do it in person. Giving feedback in writing may be easier for the manager, but it will rob the recipient of an opportunity to respond or ask for clarification.

be specific. Instead of telling a shy person he or she is doing something wrong, be specific about what was done well, what was done poorly, and what needs to be improved. Focus on a significant incident or event that illustrates a key problem that needs changing.

offer a solution. Make useful suggestions for alternatives for approaching the problem, either for the current situation or the next time it comes up.

be sensitive. With shy employees especially, you must tune into how your critique is being received. Pay close attention to body language and ask for feedback on what you are saying to make sure he or she understands and is taking it the way you intended it.

●●●

Dave Opton, founder of ExecuNet, a career-management firm for senior-level executives, suggests asking for the help of a shy employee as a way to give feedback. "In asking for them to help solve a particular issue, it doesn't direct the problem specifically at them. They may recognize that they exhibit the behavior as well, but makes it much easier to receive when it is presented in a way that makes them part of the solution rather than the centerpiece of the problem." Also tell your employee why you have asked for help. Say that you have often seen them do it properly and therefore think they would be a great role model for others to follow. "This helps to build their self-esteem and reinforce the behavior you want."

interviewing shy people

When you interview a new employee, you won't know whether they are shy before you meet them. But it's a safe bet that most of us are nervous when being interviewed by a stranger, so do what you can to increase the comfort level and help them relax. Help the interviewee see that your company and office is a safe place, and that you are an advocate rather than an interrogator. The following ideas apply to everyone, but are especially important for candidates who are shy.

Here's what Opton says to each candidate he interviews, shy or not. "I've been interviewed enough to know it's not the most comfortable situation, so I appreciate your position. Secondly, the most important thing we can do for you is to make sure we provide you with as much info as we can about who we are, how we work, what it's like to come in here every day. Because at the end of the day, it's your life you're messing around with and it's very important that you make the right decision. So I'll do everything I can do provide an honest picture of this place and there will also be time for you to ask questions." This approach should immediately relax the candidate. By letting the candidate know there will be time to ask questions, you invite him or her to prepare questions along the way, rather than putting him or her on the spot at the end with, "Do you have any questions?"

Although you interview for both skills and attitudes, it is easier to acquire and train for skills than to change someone's attitudes. With less-assertive candidates, gently probe and engage the candidate in a conversation that allows them to communicate his or her value system by offering open-ended questions so he or she can comment and expand.

ask for stories. Our brains are designed to hold stories better than facts, which means that we both tell them better and hear them better. To the question, "What was your greatest achievement at your last job?" a shy candidate may answer in as few words as possible "I increased revenue by 50%." If you want more, ask for a description or a story to help a shy person open up and expand the response.

ask *how* instead of *what*. Instead of asking for the "greatest achievement," include "and tell me how you accomplished that." Use the word "story" in your question, as in, "Tell me the story of how you accomplished this."

reveal yourself. To build rapport and make the candidate comfortable, look for an opening in the comments he or she makes or the stories he or she tells, that may trigger your own memories of similar situations. Share those to let the other person know you can empathize.

At the end, after answering any questions, let the candidate know also that if other questions come up later, as is very common, you are responsive and available by phone or e-mail.

be on the lookout for bullies at work

Bullying—using power to hurt or humiliate another—is one of the fastest-growing causes for complaints among professionals. Each year, approximately one person in five in the United States workforce faces bullying. In fact, some countries report that it is more common than racial discrimination or sexual harassment!

As a manager, it is your responsibility to make sure none of your employees are bullied. But such behavior is not always obvious. It requires your attention. Tactics may include teasing, constant criticism, insults, gossip, and unreasonable demands. The stress of bullying is created not only by what actually happens, but also by the fear of what might happen. Not all shy people are victims of bullies, but shy people are particularly susceptible to this type of stress, and therefore often the easiest targets. This is partially due to the fact that because they have trouble interacting with others, they have very little social support. Bullies won't pick on someone who has a lot of friends to help out and respond.

The best approach to bullying is called "management by walking around." Dave Opton says, "It is important if you have someone who you know might be subject to being bullied. Sort of like the police beefing up patrols in a high-crime area. It's a sad commentary, but part of a manager's job is to be a cop, only in an office setting, it is more like the community-based police station." Beyond that, if you are meeting frequently with your employees, you will know their behavior and body language well enough to know when things change or are tense and take the time to probe as to the reasons for the change.

The manager must break the cycle by showing no tolerance for bullying. Use whatever tools you can—office memos, training seminars, or a policy in place for people to report bullying. Talk to your staff about how to document bad behavior. Also, if shy employees have trouble creating a support network, step in and help out. Pair employees up on tasks and projects so they can learn to develop interdependent contact. Pair shy people with those who are more shy than themselves, so they can get a different perspective on their own behavior.

III

Communication Cheat Sheets

11

How to Say What You Mean

If the workplace was simply the place you did your work, things would be much easier. Instead, whether you work in a small office, a large corporation, or alone at home, the workplace is where we all bring ourselves and our baggage—that is, our outlook on the world, our worries, our insecurities, our fears, and so on. We all do, and this is what makes basic exchanges at work problematic.

The one thing to remember is that most of what happens at work—what we say to each other at work and the way we say it—is not about work, and has little to do with the work at hand. It may have to do with the past or something a bit more current, such as a breakfast spat, a sick child at daycare, or a baby on the way. You will probably never know.

What you can know is this: It isn't about you. Even when on the surface it's about something you did, the reaction is rarely about you, especially if it is disproportionate to the reality. That's the time to take your focus outward and bring your genuine curiosity to bear, because it's fascinating to watch people interact and try to figure out what's really going on, even if you're right in the middle of it.

Here are a few situations in which communication can be improved by using the tools and techniques you've read about throughout this book. It's not an exhaustive list, but it covers a number of situations you are likely to encounter in your workaday life.

topic: saying no

The ability to say no is crucial to success in business. It plays a role in managing, setting up realistic expectations, establishing trust, and being a professional. But we often say yes to avoid conflict or to prevent another person from getting mad, despite the fact that we know from experience that is only good for creating turmoil. A simple yes in a moment of weakness can snowball into conflict.

It is essential to know your capabilities and be clear with others about what you can and cannot do. And it's always better to under-promise and over-deliver rather than the opposite. So if you want to say yes, hold back and make it a maybe instead. And if you are able to do what needs to be done, the other person will be pleased instead of disappointed.

●●●

▶ **situation.** Someone asks a question you don't feel comfortable answering.

▶ **strategy.** There will also always be people who ask questions you don't want to answer, people who don't know what is (and isn't) appropriate. You can't stand up to them and you're not even sure why. In fact, maybe one reason for your reluctance to engage with others is so you won't have to set boundaries. Is there is a certain type of person with whom this happens regularly? Get to know yourself well enough to identify your shyness pattern and watch for it. That way, you can use the following strategies to handle these people without feeling as though you've betrayed yourself. Keep these two things in mind:

1. these people usually don't mean any harm. They may be young and eager, or simply insensitive and not used to thinking before they speak. As a result, what comes out may be inappropriate in itself, or just bad timing. Either way, take a moment to consider the purpose before you respond.

2. you don't have to answer. Your responsibility is to take care of yourself, and often that simply means saying no comment. A few ways to say that include, "I'd rather not answer that question," or "Why do you ask?" deflecting the question back on to him or her. If they still don't get it, be direct. "I'm not comfortable answering that question." They usually jump back and get the picture.

●●●

▶**situation.** Someone asks you to meet at a time that isn't convenient.

▶**strategy.** This depends on why the time doesn't work for you but keep in mind that you don't have to automatically say yes, even if it's your boss. Try offering a time that would be more convenient for you, without ruling out the possibility of complying to the request. For example: In response to "Can you meet Friday at 11?" you can say, "Monday would be better. My morning is wide open."

This response implies that if your preference can't be accommodated, you could do it at the suggested time. But if you ask for what works best for you first, you won't feel pushed around.

●●●

▶ **situation.** How to disagree with someone who has power over you

▶ **strategy.** Some of us perceive any potential disagreement as a confrontation, which it often is not. Instead of disagreeing, we stay silent. There are many disadvantages to this strategy, including the fact that a good solution to whatever problem is at hand may not be found just because we don't speak up. Disagreement is an aspect of healthy communication, and it gets more and more comfortable with practice. Without practice, however, it remains in your mind as confrontation.

In fact, the problem arises not when you disagree, but how you do it. Conversations don't usually accelerate into confrontations unless you disagree in a way that provokes the other. And although you can't control another person, you can control yourself and your reactions. Here are seven approaches to experiment with:

1. begin with a positive, rather than a negative. Say, "Yes, and…." Then find what you agree with and comment on that first. Then add your contribution.

2. don't be abrasive. After acknowledging the other person's point of view, present yours neutrally, as one of many options. If possible, draw connections between the other person's perspective and your own.

3. show that you respect his or her position. Instead of saying, "I disagree with you," you might say, "In my opinion..." or, " It seems to me that..." or, "May I share a different perspective?" Show humility and the other person will honor you by allowing you to speak freely.

4. stay focused on the issue at hand. Don't be distracted by the person's attitude or tone, which you can't control.

5. put it in writing. If you cannot disagree in person or in front of a group, let the important person know you have a different opinion, and put it in writing to clarify your thoughts.

6. know when to defer. If your job is on the line, keep things in perspective and know when to let go. What's important is not whether you win, but that you speak up.

7. seek to understand first, then to be understood. Listen first, but make sure you get the floor to speak as well.

topic: avoiding miscommunication

It may not come most naturally, but keeping the lines of communication open is one of the best ways to avoid miscommunication. It's tempting to avoid people you aren't ready to talk to because you haven't yet done what needs to be done, or don't have the answer to their question. But keeping others in the dark is the more serious offense and can lead to problems that result from their imaginings. You'll be amazed at how many mistakes you avoid and problems you head off by reaching out and keeping people up to date on where you are with a project or a process.

If you're working on an ongoing project, schedule a regular 10-minute conference call to apprise those involved of the status of a project and get any questions answered. That way, with a regular meeting on the calendar, you won't have to start from scratch to find a time or place to meet.

●●●

▶ **situation.** You need help but don't want to ask.

People often avoid asking for help for all sorts of reasons, such as:

- You are embarrassed that you need assistance. You believe that asking for help indicates weakness.

- You think that asking will open you up to criticism.

- You think that even if you ask for it, you won't get it.

- You think there will be strings attached.

- You believe no one has time to help.

- You think that even if they do, it won't be done right. "I'll just do it myself."

But in reality, you are extremely limited by what you can accomplish on your own.

▶ **strategy.** Ask for help.

be direct. Don't hint around and hope the other person will volunteer to help you. Let him know exactly what you need and how long it will take. Acknowledge his workload and time constraints. Give all the details and then let him respond with yes or no.

hand over the power. Don't demand help. People push back automatically if not given a choice. Instead, say, "I'm in a pickle," or "I have a problem," or "I have a really urgent need. I hope you can help me." That puts the other person in a position of power and often makes them want to say yes, or at least consider your request.

prepare thoroughly. Provide all the information necessary to help you. For example, if you've asked a former client to serve as a reference, provide her with a copy of your bio or resume, a brief description of the project at hand, and the name of anyone who may call.

offer to return the favor. Your contacts will be more motivated to help you if you seek ways to assist them and are responsive to their requests. Even if your help is not needed, your offer will be appreciated.

always say thanks. Acknowledge all efforts done on your behalf with a thank-you note in the mail. This has quite a strong impact. Also, send a little token of your appreciation, such as a music CD or a business book that might be applicable.

●●●

▶**situation.** You are behind on a project and can't make your deadline.

▶ **strategy.** Speaking up sooner rather than later affords you more options than just waiting and hoping that things will be fine. Address the issue with a focus on the solutions rather than the deadline problem. Offer a few options, and then let your client or supervisor make the decision. That way, you are covered and have done your job.

●●●

▶ **situation.** You are pulled off a project

▶ **strategy.** Take the time to let those involved know. Change without warning, and therefore without preparation, is not smoothly handled by most people. If something is about to change and you are involved, avoid surprise by giving as much advance warning as possible. Think about how others would want to be advised of the change. Who should tell them? How? By phone, e-mail, or in person? This depends on the magnitude of the change, but e-mail should be the last choice. In person is the first choice, but when that's not possible, do it on the phone.

Here's what the people involved in the change need to know:

● What has happened

● How it affects the project

● What your response is

● How your response may affect their responsibilities

● What needs to happen in your opinion to finish the job in your absence

●●●

" " *I was working on the revised edition of* PR *for* Dummies *with one of the company editors. Near the end of the process, I submitted almost all of the final material, but I didn't hear back from her, which was unusual, but I didn't think much of it. When I made the final submission a week later, I got a message back saying, 'As you probably already know, because of some scheduling changes, one of our freelance editors has taken over this project for me.'*

This was the first I'd heard and, needless to say, I was surprised to hear the news and even more surprised to hear it this way. I immediately picked up the phone and asked, 'Is it true that you're not on the project anymore?'

'Yes, didn't the new editor call you?' she asked.

I didn't say this but wanted to: 'And even if she had, that's not who I should be hearing it from. You are the one I have the relationship with. And if the relationship is changing, it should come from you. And it wouldn't have been overkill if your boss had been in the loop too.'"

—Eric Yaverbaum, coauthor
PR for Dummies

prepare yourself for tough conversations

Because you can't avoid tough conversations, you'll have to prepare for them. This worksheet will help you clarify your goals, get your thoughts on paper, and keep you on track if things don't go as you hope.

●●●

issue. State the problem clearly from your point of view.

_____

_____

_____.

goal. What is your ideal outcome? _____

_____

_____.

outcome. What is the worse case scenario? What outcomes will be acceptable to you?_____

_____

_____

_____

_____.

main points. What do you need to say to arrive at your ideal possible outcome?_____

_____

_____

_____

_____.

pitfalls. What could derail the communications? What will you do if the person becomes emotional? What questions could be asked that you are not prepared to answer? Prepare a response for those situations._____

_____

_____

_____.

next steps. What will you do next? What do you need the other person to do? How will you follow up to resolve the issue? _____

_____

_____

_____.

●●●

▶**situation.** Dealing with a difficult client or colleague.

First of all, people aren't difficult—but relationships are. It's the dynamic between two people that makes an interaction either difficult or harmonious. To prove this, you have simply to watch someone you perceive as difficult relating to other people. It's unlikely he or she has trouble with absolutely everyone. So what is it about you and what happens between you that causes a reaction in the other person? And vice versa? This is what you can be curious about.

▶**strategy.** From that curious point of view, watch that person interacting with others and see what's different. If you can see the difficult person in another way, you might behave differently with them. And although you can't control the difficult person, you can experiment with your behavior, and you are half of the equation.

learn what you can and cannot control. Focus on what you can control in this situation. That is essential.

do a lot of listening. Listen for the underlying issue, for the buried emotions beneath. With difficult people, it's best to keep your distance and stay as objective and empathetic as possible.

don't fight. Instead, look for the openings in the other person's point of view. Look for where he or she may be willing to bend. Then guide him or her that way.

let them know you are on his or her side. Many people are difficult because they feel alone. If you can let customers know you are with them, they may not be quite as difficult.

stay out of their way. If the customer is really difficult, interact only when you must; otherwise stay out of the way.

●●●

▶**situation.** How to handle offensive interviewers.

▶**strategy.** First of all, keep everything in perspective. If an interviewer is offensive, consider whether you even want to work with the person or company. If a question seems out of line, don't respond right away. Ask for clarification to make sure you're hearing the question correctly. If in fact it is offensive, you can say you'd rather not answer. Bring in your curiosity and try to read between the lines. Why would this person be asking this question? Sometimes, an offensive question or comment is asked to elicit a response and to see how you react in a stressful or critical situation.

Try turning a negative into a positive. For example, an interviewer may say, "If I were to tell you that you had no future with our organization, nor do you have the ability to succeed in this position, how would you feel?" Don't be alarmed—it's a leading question. He said "If..." so it's a hypothetical situation and does not reflect how the interviewer feels at a given point and time. Then answer also with a hypothetical: "If you were to tell me that I had no future in with your organization, I would ask you what part of my qualifications suggest that I could not succeed in this position, and I would revisit, clarify, or improve those areas so I could meet the job requirements."

●●●

▶ **situation.** How to handle an irate customer.

▶ **strategy.** When dealing with an irate customer, your first task is to convince him or her that you're on his or her side. Only after an angry customer believes that you understand his problem and sympathize with his plight will he be willing to believe that you really mean to help him. After you've expressed your concern, use the customer's name in making a promise to help. Say, "Mr. Jones, I fully intend to help you," or something similar, after he's calmed down enough to listen to you. This will go a long way toward making him cooperative. Finally, never come back with nothing. Even if his expectations are unrealistic, give him something for his troubles. Even if it's something insubstantial, if it's given as the best you can—after genuinely going to bat for him—he may be mollified. (Reprinted with permission from Early To Rise *www.earlytorise.com*)

● ● ●

▶ **situation.** You're being bullied by someone in your office. It's not always easy to break free of bullies, because they don't usually start off by bullying you. At first, bullies are often charming. He or she will get you to like him or her and before long, you'll do anything not to disagree or offend.

▶ **strategy.** If this is happening to you, whether the bully is a client, your boss, or a coworker, Susan Lipkins, author of *Preventing Hazing: How Parents, Teachers and Coaches Can Stop the Violence, Harassment, and Humiliation*, offers these suggestions to stop being the victim:

- The single most important piece of information to keep in mind is that you have power and that you are choosing to give up your power to the bully; you do not have to. The bully will not hurt you, he will simply find another victim.

- Your desire to be liked by the bully, or protected by him (or her), is putting you in the position of victim.

- The bully knows how to intimidate and manipulate.

- If you do not take care of yourself, stand up for yourself, who will?

- Small wins are better than none.

●●●

I have always been shy with my over-bearing boss —doing more than my share of work just to keep her out of my hair. Last summer, I was particularly burdened by additional work (much of which was outside of my job-description) and she was pressing me throughout the day to get a project to her. I had other high-priority items for the firm partners. So in response to one too many requests, I cracked. I said, 'Stop pushing me around'—though I think it came out more like 'Get off my back!' She instantly backed down, surprised at my outburst. I think this confrontation was heard by one of the partners so the unexpected result was that a new person was hired to assist me with the not-my-job-description work. Plus, my boss has been very nice to me, now dropping items in my in-box and withdrawing— usually silently."

—David Tornabene

●●●

▶**situation.** You've made a mistake.

No matter how much you may try to avoid mistakes, they are inevitable. In reality, mistakes are not the problem. How you handle them is much more significant in the long run. But it's difficult to deal with mistakes maturely when you're busy feeling bad, guilty, anxious, or afraid about how someone will react.

▶**strategy.** Bring your mistake quickly to the attention of others with the simple preface, "I've made a mistake." Then do what you can to prevent consequences and diminish negative (and often costly) effects on yourself and on others.

●●●

▶**situation.** You've offended a colleague without knowing it.

▶**strategy.** You can't control how other people hear and react to what you say. If you suspect that you might have offended someone, acknowledge it with, " If I offended you in any way when I [said, did, did not say, did not do] something, I'd like to apologize." From there:

1. offer an explanation. Explain your thinking (or lack of thinking) process to help the other person understand your point of view.

2. be curious about how it was perceived. Use the opportunity to learn a little bit about that person.

3. ask what you can do to resolve the issue. Though you can't take back what you did or said, ask what you can do to make the person feel better. Be creative and take the initiative to offer suggestions as to what you can do to minimize the results of your mistake.

4. keep it all in perspective. Usually we panic in the moment regarding something that, looking back, we realize is not that significant. Try to bring that hindsight into the present moment. If you handle this well, it's likely that your relationship will improve.

●●●

" *In my first career as a Navy pilot, I developed a biting sense of humor that was very common for that environment. After I left the Navy, however, I quickly found that type of humor did not play well at all in the outside world! I really caused some ruffled feathers and hurt feelings with my one-liners. In addition to learning to control my tongue, I also had to learn to apologize to those I offended. This took some trial and error, but one of my most effective tactics went something like this: 'You know, I said something to you that came out very differently than what I actually meant. My wife is working with me on this, but I'm concerned that I offended you, which is the last thing I wanted to do. I am very sorry—what can I do to make it right?' I'm always sincere when I say it, and I think the words I use convey that. Also, asking them that last question puts them in a position to offer forgiveness (if they want) without feeling like a victim. I can't claim credit for the idea (I had help), but I can say it works!"*

—John Withers

●●●

▶**situation.** You're trying to reach someone and all you get is silence

▶**strategy.** Be persistent. Don't interpret silence as rejection, and don't be discouraged. There can be so many reasons why someone doesn't respond right away. Maybe he didn't receive your message, or maybe she accidentally deleted it. Perhaps he or she meant to respond but got overwhelmed by other issues. When it comes to those who don't know you well, don't even expect a response to your first outreach. Plan your communication strategy to include a second outreach a day or two later.

simple strategies to get people to respond

You don't want to be a pest, yet you want to stay in touch. But how often is too often to reach out? The line between persistence and pest is a thin one, and it's a moving target. In other words, it depends on the day, on the person, on his or her need, and many other things you won't even get wind of. There are many different ways to deal with the silence. Here are some of the strategies recommended by the readers of *Quick Tips from Marketing Mentor*:

- Be patient and persistent.
- Ask for a yea or nay.
- Send a real letter via snail mail.
- Ask if they're okay. Concern on your part may motivate them to respond.
- Give a deadline to respond.

- Put "second request" in the subject line.

- Keep calling without leaving messages until you reach a person live. Try calling early or later in the business day.

- Ask if he or she got your first (or recent) message.

- Ask a simple question that is easy to respond to.

- Develop an automatic keep-in-touch system, such as a monthly newsletter or e-zine, to make sure that your name is in the forefront of his or her mind.

●●●

▶ **situation.** What if your client or boss doesn't respond and it's important?

▶ **strategy.**

- Devise a strategy based on what you know of your boss or client's communication preferences and habits.

- Approach with curiosity. Ask if he or she is aware of the issue and its priority.

- Ask if it's a priority to him or her. Sometimes being sympathetic to the other person's position is a wise strategy.

- Ask what the obstacle is. You may not be aware of details in the process that may be getting in the way, such as someone who needs to give approval but also isn't responding.

● Ask what you can do to help move the process forward. Can you provide additional info, do some homework, make a call or two, or somehow eliminate the obstacle?

To avoid this type of situation, you can set this strategy with your boss at the beginning of your employment with the company. Share a scenario and ask how he or she likes to be alerted.

What to Say in All Sorts of Situations

You're asked a question and your mind goes blank. You're looking at the other person, but what's in front of you becomes blurry. The spotlight is on you, and you don't want to say the wrong thing. You're racking your brain for something to say. But nothing comes. What should you do? All that worry about what to say is wasted, because the truth is, most people don't listen very well. Think of all the times when you space out and your mind wanders. We're all doing that almost involuntarily. So keep that in mind every time you struggle with what to say, and as you experiment with these ideas.

topic: office politics

▶ **situation.** Someone promised but didn't follow through. Many of us make promises right and left, but many of those details fall through the cracks, even when written down. That is a fact of doing business.

▶ **strategy.** Don't take everything at face value. On a case by case basis, determine how reliable the person is.

If you don't know them, take all offers with a grain of salt and keep your expectations low. If what's been offered is something you really want or need, remind the person about it gently by saying, "That was really great idea you had earlier about (blank) and I would really appreciate reading the article you mentioned. Do you want me to send a reminder e-mail about it?" If, however, what you were promised is a big deal, such as a new assignment or a raise, it is your responsibility to find out what happened. Give your client or supervisor an idea about what you'd like to discuss. Do this in writing, not in an offhand way. Demonstrate the seriousness by being professional about it.

To get into the conversation, open by stating your understanding of the situation and asking if it is accurate. If so, proceed by asking whether anything has changed since then to affect your new assignment (or raise, vacation, benefit, promotion, and so on). Approach this from a position of curiosity, instead of entitlement. Stay calm and do as much as you can to understand the position of the other person.

●●●

▶ **situation.** You think or imagine you've done something wrong.

▶ **strategy.** Don't torture yourself. If you sense someone is unhappy with something you've done, it is your right (and obligation) to find out. Otherwise, you'll waste a lot of time worrying! Whether it's a client, coworker, or supervisor, you'll be better off if you initiate the conversation rather than waiting for the other person to approach you. It may have nothing to do with you, and then again it might. Either way, it's best to find out.

In broaching the topic, your people reading skills will come in handy. Keep your eyes open for a time when the other person is open. Then keep the focus on you by saying, "I have a question for you." Or, "I've been wondering about something and wanted to get your point of view." Don't add mystery by saying, "We need to talk." This often sends another person into his or her worst nightmares. Then, notice the person's reaction, however slight. Does he avert his eyes? Is there a slight stress in his voice? Does he step back or put his hands in his pockets? None of these mean anything in and of themselves, but they are important to observe as part of the whole message.

If the answer is yes, there is a problem, describe the situation from your perspective without being defensive. Let the other person know you did your best and discuss together how could you have done better. Ask what other resources you should be aware of. Approach it as a problem-solving discussion about the future. Don't focus on the past.

If the answer is no, and it's clear you were imagining the problem, don't make a big deal about it and don't be embarrassed. Do not, in relief, open up and tell the person what you had imagined. Doing so will give them too much information that may be used later. Instead, use the experience to learn your own behavior pattern better so that next time you'll be able to tell when you're being paranoid.

●●●

▶ **situation.** You have your eye on a project but don't know how to ask for it.

▶ **strategy.** Identify and express your preference for the types of projects you are interested in. At the beginning of a planning cycle, let your manager know which ideas interest you most, or what you'd most like to work on and learn from. You can do this in writing or verbally. You may need to remind him or her later. Don't assume that just because you've said it, it was heard or remembered.

●●●

▶ **situation.** Someone in the office is gossiping.

▶ **strategy.** First of all, don't participate in office gossip. As for the others, you can't ask people not to gossip, but you can change the subject or let them know how you feel about it by simply saying, "I'm uncomfortable with this conversation." You will also build trust by making it clear that you will not gossip. Others will feel safe and will be more likely to open up to you. At the same time, don't judge others for gossiping. Instead be curious about what they get from it.

●●●

▶ **situation.** Someone is gossiping about you.

▶ **strategy.** Before jumping to conclusions, approach the gossiper with curiosity. Tell him or her what you heard and ask if it's true. Listen to the explanation, which may be defensive, and try to understand the motivation. Then, simply let the person know how it affects you, which they may be unaware of.

topic: speaking up in a group

Staff meetings or any small group situation can be a nightmare for the less assertive. Maybe it's the size of the group or the presence of a particular person. Whatever the reason, noticing your patterns and working around them will make it easier to speak up.

●●●

▶ **situation.** You're afraid you'll sound stupid if you speak up.

▶ **strategy.** It's so tempting to relax into silence. You may even decide before a meeting that you won't be participating. Shift your attention from yourself to what you may have to contribute. It is through participation that we learn, by asking questions and commenting on what doesn't make sense. Asking for clarification shows you are listening, interested, and willing to speak up. And so what if you feel stupid? There are always others who are as confused but won't say so. If you do, others will be grateful.

●●●

▶ **situation.** You want to speak up, but everyone's talking at once.

▶ **strategy.** A simple phrase can help here too. "I have a thought I'd like to share," or, "I have something to add," will get the attention of others and give you the time and space to share your thoughts. Sometimes, even if you don't contribute verbally, you can use body language to communicate your participation. Nod your head and make eye contact to indicate you're following the conversation.

Don't lean back in your chair, doodle, or look off into space, even if you're listening. Another way of participating is to volunteer to take notes. That way you're active, but not required to speak up. You can also add your ideas to the notes afterward.

> *It was too uncomfortable for me to be sitting at a luncheon table with 8 people. I realized early on that I had to be giving the speech, not hearing it. To me, that's much safer than walking into a room of strangers where I had to introduce myself and make small talk. The nice thing about public speaking is that it's a controlled environment. I have my script, and my PowerPoint. It's my material so I know it inside out. Plus, standing behind the podium certifies me as an expert, whether I feel that way or not. After the speech, people come up and talk about my topic, which is comfortable because I know my topic."*
> —Sheila Campbell

6 tips for presenting your ideas

If you want to move up the corporate ladder or increase your company's visibility, presentation skills are essential. But you can't present in front of a group when you can barely raise your hand in a meeting.

Don't adopt someone else's style. Instead, take the time to develop your own personal style, adapting what you like from others. Don't discount a quiet style. In fact, when you speak quietly, people listen more closely. Some of the most effective presenters speak in very low, calm, and authoritative voices.

In *Power and Persuasion*, author Michael Masterson advises memorizing the first and last lines of your presentation but nothing else. "The speaker who reads his speech is sure to fail. He can't make eye contact. He can't become passionate in any genuine way. He can't light up his audience. You need a strong first sentence or three. (These are the lines that you are giving to individuals, with eye contact and a smile.) And you need a strong closing line so your audience knows when to applaud, but in between you need to speak strongly from the heart."

Here are some tips on presenting, whether it's a two-minute project update or a 15-minute presentation of your new ideas:

1. prepare. Do your homework and know your audience so you can make it all about them. If you're presenting to a group of strangers, spend some time in advance getting to know a few of them. Find out what questions they have and be prepared to answer them.

2. create an outline. Instead of reading verbatim from a speech, use PowerPoint or note cards to outline your talk. The phrases should be simple reminders of an idea. Rehearse using the reminders to trigger the story or idea.

3. relax by taking a few deep breaths. Stop thinking about your presentation and banish perfectionism from your mind. Trust that you know all you're going to know for today and focus your attention on what's right in front of you. This will help you when you are in front of the audience.

4. warm up. Before a presentation, don't isolate yourself. Use the time to get to know the audience. Sit with attendees, if appropriate. This will also let them know you are accessible, which will affect how they receive your presentation, how involved they get, and how closely they pay attention.

5. speak as you would one-on-one. Build rapport with an audience one person at a time. Speak your first sentence while looking at one person. Then look at another. Make eye contact with someone you know or someone who seems friendly. Smile. Notice their reactions and respond to them. If one person is confused, others might be too. If the audience is involved (characterized by nodding and smiling,) stay with them.

6. be a vessel, not the source. Take the pressure off yourself by thinking about yourself as the vessel through which the information is passing, not the source of it.

topic: socializing

Whether you enjoy it or not, socializing is part of the work world, whether you attend a business luncheon with a client or you're taken out to dinner by a vendor. You may hate this type of thing, but if you want to expand your network and develop strong relationships that support your career growth, socializing is part of it. Don't expect to hit it off with everyone. You'll get along well with some, and not so well with others. Either way, it helps to have some social skills to bring to bear on the different kinds of situations that follow.

●●●

▶ **situation.** You're seated next to a VIP.

▶ **strategy.** Treat the VIP as you would any coworker. You may be a little more careful of what you say, but you don't have to make a big impression. It's enough to introduce yourself or, if you've already met, remind her of who you are and what you're working on. Before saying goodbye, ask if you can stay in touch to ask a question or keep her current of what you're working on. That way, you don't have to depend on this one moment to make an impression. Instead you have used it to obtain permission to make a stronger impression over time, in essence to develop a relationship with this person.

●●●

▶**situation.** The holiday office party.

▶**strategy.** Use it as another opportunity to get to know those you work with. Prepare a few questions and issues to discuss or, for more general topics of conversation, something from the news that has affected you. Make an effort to approach people you might not have access to otherwise, colleagues in other departments, or anyone you may not see regularly, such as top management or employees from other locations. Use the time to begin building, or continue strengthening, your relationships.

Don't drink too much, even if it's open bar. You may be uncomfortable, but this is not the time or the place to loosen up with alcohol. Know your limit and stop before you get there. And if you bring your spouse or partner along, prepare him or her with some information about who's who, and introduce him or her around. Remind your partner not to lobby for you or confront people you have complained about.

●●●

▶ **situation.** You attend an out-of-town conference where you don't know anyone.

▶ **strategy.** Preconnect. Find out if any of your clients or colleagues will be attending. Make plans in advance so you have a social agenda in place when you arrive. During the conference, think about ideas or questions that can carry over into discussion or debate later on. Which ones did you agree with or disagree with? Even if you're not actively looking for work, don't miss out on opportunities to make good connections for the future. In fact, when you are not in need is the best time to do so. This will let others know you are interested in them out of genuine interest, not out of need. You'll be more comfortable, more relaxed and that will not go unnoticed. Always take notes at conferences that you can share with others at the next meeting. Knowledge is a commodity that is worth sharing with your peers and your boss.

questions to ask at a conference

● What was one of the best things your company did this year?

● We had trouble with so-and-so last quarter, did you?

● What's the newest thing you're working on? What's new on your list? Which projects did you finish last year? What's a day at the office like for you now?

● How does this convention compare to the last one? Are there other people from your firm here? Did you bring your family along?

Hot topics in the news are always good—scan the Internet or the newspaper for headlines. But stay away from politics, religion, or anything controversial. This is not the time or place.

▶ **situation.** A coworker is flirting with you.

▶ **strategy.** Keep the flirting to a minimum. Be aware that boundaries can sometimes blur on unfamiliar turf. Behavior rules of the office apply outside as well. Don't get swept away by someone who's paying attention to you because they're away from home. It could mean trouble later.

●●●

I've always had difficulty at conferences. So many people and networking opportunities, but I never know what to say and how to say it at the right time to the right people who could help me the most. I either avoid them altogether, or I make small talk, but not smart talk. During a critique once, I was so nervous I chatted about everything unrelated, and not about what I needed help with. I'm slowly overcoming my anxiety by being better prepared and having a list of questions and objectives with me. After I receive information I need, I become more relaxed and I'm able to enjoy the conference enough to start interacting and networking with other attendees."

—Cynthia Smith

topic: money

Shy people hate talking about money or asking for money—they commonly say that it feels as if they are begging. Talking about fees or salary can get you caught in the web of self-worth, when it is not related to that at all. The real issue is what is fair compensation for your efforts?

Your time, skills, intellect, creativity, past experience, and efforts have a certain value to you. They also have a certain value to the person with whom you are negotiating a fee, price, or salary. The goal is to find the overlap between the value you place, and the value he or she places. If there is no overlap, you have no conversation. If you want $100 per hour to make follow-up calls, and your prospect can't afford that, or doesn't value the effort that highly, they won't pay it—no matter how much you're worth it. It has nothing to do with your self-worth.

●●●

▶ **situation.** You don't know how to broach the topic of money.

▶ **strategy.** Be direct and simply say, "Let's talk about money." Always ask for the other person to tell you what he or she has in mind first. The other person may not have anything in mind, but sometimes they will, and it will give you a place to start. From there you can either tell your prospect or supervisor what you want and let him or her respond. Once your positions are out in the open, don't feel pressured to respond immediately. Take time to think. Whatever you do, don't rush into any decisions. This may convey desperation or over-eagerness, neither of which are positions of strength. Also, if talking about money is one of a number of issues being discussed with this person, create a simple agenda for the meeting and put "money" on the list of things to discuss. That way, when you get there, you don't feel as though you're bringing it up out of the blue.

●●●

▶ **situation.** Deadbeat clients aren't paying their bills

▶ **strategy.** Don't let yourself be pushed around by people who owe you money and are counting on the fact that you won't pester them. Set up a system whereby you contact them regularly and remind them of what they owe. Sometimes they'll pay just to get you off their back. If that doesn't work, consider whether it's worth your time to take legal action. More important, learn what you can from the experience about which clients to avoid.

●●●

❝ *With one client who hasn't paid, and I'm pretty sure they're dealing with a cash-flow issue, I'm proposing different payment options. That way, I show that I'm flexible and want to help them as a customer, but I'm still getting my point across: I need payment.*"

—Mistina Bates

●●●

▶ **situation.** How to ask for money upfront.

▶ **strategy.** First of all, this is business, and asking for a deposit on an order or a project conveys professionalism. If you don't do it, you come across as an amateur. As for how to ask, frame it as any business would. "We have a policy that requires 30 percent of the fee paid in advance. Once we secure the deposit, we will begin work." Say it clearly and unapologetically. If your client or prospect doesn't want to pay up front, you can consider negotiating another arrangement but, especially if you've never worked together before, neglecting to get an advance puts your company in a weak position, with no leverage, when the unexpected happens.

topic: negotiating successful agreements

There are plenty of negotiating books out there (two of the best include *Getting to Yes* by Roger Fisher and WilliamUry and *Starting with No* by Jim Camp). But for many of us, the problem in negotiations has to do with speaking up and asking for what we deserve. Again, preparation is the key. Set aside the time to think through and write down as many scenarios as you can think of. Then role-play in your mind how you would handle each one. Once you've done your preparation, not only will you feel more comfortable, but you'll have strategies ready to deal with almost anything that can come up. Here are two useful preparation tips:

1. **don't negotiate with a stranger.** In order to do effective preparation, you need to know with whom you're dealing. This is especially important when the stakes are high. Even if time only allows for a short getting-acquainted phone call, insist on it rather than going into the negotiation cold.

2. **rank your requests or issues in order of difficulty.** Get your partner agreeing by starting with the easiest issues on your agenda (such as the deadline). Get agreement on the simple things before you move to financial issues, which often require more finesse.

●●●

▶ **situation.** It's time to raise your fees

▶ **strategy.** If you have a long-time and loyal client who is still paying your low fees, let her know how far you've come since you initially agreed to that fee, what others are paying for the same services or products, and how you'd like to bring them up to speed. Don't make the increase arbitrary. Create a policy that calls for annual or biannual increases. Say, "We value your business and we would like to continue with you in the future. However, we cannot do this without increasing your fees to come more in line with what others are currently paying." Always offer the option to say no and move on. You may have outgrown each other, and neither has had the courage to address that issue.

●●●

▶ **situation.** It's time for your annual review.

▶ **strategy.** Before you head off into a negotiation for your annual review, here are five things you should keep in mind.

1. prepare. An annual review is a high-pressure situation. Prepare an outline of the points you want to make and the questions you have.

2. understand the grading system. An annual review is not a report card. It's important to understand the scale on which you're being evaluated. So ask in advance. Just because you don't "exceed expectations" doesn't mean you haven't done well.

3. describe your best accomplishments. If you've accomplished your goals, it's up to you to show how you've done so. This isn't bragging. Bring a list of your achievements. Describe what's gone well, what's been challenging, what you're working on, and where you need help. Don't ignore your mistakes. Instead, show what you've learned from them and, if possible, how you've already integrated those lessons.

4. know what needs improvement. Take a balanced view and be ready to answer the question: "In what areas do you think you need the most improvement?"

5. know what next step you want. Even if a promotion isn't imminent, be sure each year moves you ahead a step or two. Make it clear that your intention in the review is to see where you've been and where you're going. Don't let your supervisor leave the room without committing (or at least agreeing) to the next step. Show interest in growing within the company and ask to meet again in six months.

●●●

▶**situation.** You didn't get the raise you expected.

▶**strategy.** Prepare by researching average salaries for your position to put your raise into perspective. Then schedule an appointment to discuss the issue. Don't have the conversation without your boss's full attention and your full preparation. During the meeting, be curious. Ask why the raise was what it was, whether it was in line with that of others, and whether you're doing a good job in your boss's eyes. Listen to the responses. If appropriate, ask if there is any way it can be increased. Cite your research about standard salaries. Remind your boss of past positive performance reviews. Provide quantifiable specifics about the value you bring every day. Advocate for yourself, but think about your performance in the context of what it means to your boss. Be careful about conveying a sense of entitlement. Don't say, "I deserve more," or "Others would value me." And don't issue ultimatums.

If more money is not an option, negotiate for other benefits, such as more vacation, a better office, and so on. As a last resort, get a commitment on the next raise or pay period, and a time frame within which it can be reassessed. If the reason you didn't get the raise you expected is due to an inadequacy in your performance, you need to know that. Ask whether, if those improvements are made, you will get the raise, and secure a commitment on that.

●●●

> *I tend to get shy when it comes to negotiating for more money on a project that has exceeded its original scope. I always have a contract for the scope of work, but for some reason when the terms of the contract have been reached, and work is still yet to be done, I get all tongue-tied trying to explain to a client that I've done the three rounds of revisions to the logo (or whatever the design project is at hand) and if they want me to continue revising, they need to pay me hourly at the rate outlined in the contract. I guess I don't want my clients to think I'm nickel-and-diming them. But why is it so hard for me to set these standard professional parameters?"*
> —Julia Reich

●●●

▶**situation.** A project has exceeded its budget and you have to tell the client it will cost more.

▶**strategy.** The problem is usually that this comes as a surprise to the client. So whenever possible, start the warning process early. That could mean highlighting when he or she signs the contract that if the scope goes beyond what is outlined, there will be an extra charge. There is usually less emotion involved if it's a hypothetical situation.

As soon as you see a problem coming up, let the client know. If possible, give them a choice as to how to handle it. For example, let him know this is the second of three revisions included in the contract, and that the next one is the last. State the obvious if necessary. Then, when the last one comes around and it's still not finished, you've already laid the groundwork and it's not a surprise. At that point, offer a couple of options about how it can be handled and provide an estimate of how much more money and time is involved.

●●●

▶**situation.** A clients asks how much a project will cost and you don't know.

▶**strategy.** It's important to be straightforward about money, but not before you have all the information to determine your fees. Don't blurt out numbers just because someone asks for a price. If the prospect or client insists, provide a range for your fees, but don't give a fixed number until you have all the information you need to come up with that number. When you are ready and you give your fee, say, "Based on the scope of these specifications" — and reiterate the scope. And don't defend your fees, especially if the client doesn't ask for an explanation.

▶ **situation.** Dealing with success.

How to handle being listened to when you speak up. If you're accustomed to feeling pushed around and not listened to, you may not recognize a positive response when you speak up.

▶ **strategy.** What are your expectations of being listened to? There is a difference between speaking up with the expectation that you will be heard and speaking up with the expectation that you won't. Clearly, we will speak more effectively if we do so with a positive expectation. And we will be much more positively received.

●●●

> " *In my new job, I am having the unexpected experience of people caring what I say and think. A problem will come up and we will all talk about it, and my boss and my colleagues are not only listening to me, but they are also deferring to my judgment. It shouldn't be a surprise; I have a lot of experience and knowledge. But for whatever reason—my childhood, family of origin, previous experiences—I almost never expect to be listened to. And now I'm being listened to on a regular basis and I'm totally freaked out. So whatever the reasons are that keep a person from speaking up, it doesn't have to be that way for the rest of one's life. The workplace may parallel a family in structure (the boss as parent, colleagues as siblings), but this 'family' can interact and work differently than the family a person grew up with.* "
> —Managing Editor
> of a Diocesan Newspaper

Recommended Reading

Allen, Scott and David Teten. *The Virtual Handshake: Opening Doors And Closing Deals Online.* New York: AMACOM, 2005.

Beckwith, Harru. *Selling the Invisible: A Field Guide to Modern Marketing.* New York: Warner Business Books, 1997.

Bly, Bob. *Webster's New World Letter Writing Handbook.* New York: Webster's New World, 2003.

Ferrazi, Keith. *Never Eat Alone.* New York: Doubleday, 2005.

Gitomer, Jeffrey. *The Little Red Book of Selling: 12.5 Principles of Sales Greatness*. Marietta, GA: Bard Press, 2004.

Godin, Seth. *The Big Moo*. New York: Portfolio Hardcover, 2005.

Keleman, Stanley. *Emotional Anatomy: The Structure of Experience*. Berkeley, CA: Center Press, 1986.

Laney, Marti Olson. *The Introvert Advantage*. New York: Workman Publishing, 2002.

Lerner, Marcy. *Vault Guide to Schmoozing*. New York: Vault, Inc., 2001.

Levy, Benjamin. *Remember Every Name Every Time*. New York: Fireside, 2002.

Nierenberg, Andrea. *Nonstop Networking*. Sterling, VA: Capital Books, 2002.

Pink, Daniel. *A Whole New Mind*. New York: Riverhead Trade, 2006.

Ratey, John J., *A User's Guide to the Brain*. New York: Vintage, 2002.

Taylor, Susan L. *In The Spirit*. New York: Harper, 1994.

Weiss, Donald H. *Why Didn't I Say That?! What to Say & How to Say It in Tough Situations on the Job*. New York: American Management Association, 1996.

Yudkin, Marcia. *Persuading on Paper*. West Conshohocken, PA: Infinity Publishing, 2002.

Works Consulted

chapter 1

Carducci, Bernardo. *Shyness: A Bold New Approach*. New York: Harper Collins, 2000.

Goleman, Daniel. *Emotional Intelligence*. New York: Bantam, 1995.

Krech, Gregg. *Naikan: Gratitude, Grace and the Japanese Art of Self-Reflection*. Berkeley, CA: Stone Bridge Press, 2001.

chapter 2

Reynolds, David. *Constructive Living*. Honolulu, HI: University of Hawaii Press, 1984.

Batchelor, Stephem. *Buddhism Without Beliefs*. New York: Riverhead Trade, 1998.

209

chapter 3

Dimitrius, JoAnn and Marc Mazzarella. *Reading People: How to Understand People and Predict Their Behavior—Anytime, Anyplace.* New York: Ballantine Books, 1999.

chapter 5

Zeldin, Theodore. *Conversation: How Talk Can Change Our Lives.* Mahwah, NJ: HiddenSpring Press, 2000.

chapter 8

Gladwell, Malcolm. *The Tipping Point.* New York: Little, Brown, 2002.

chapter 9

Murphy, Thomas. *Successful Selling for Introverts.* Shelton, CT: Thomas Murphy Sales & Marketing, 1999.

chapter 11

Lipkins, Susan. *Preventing Hazing:How Parents, Teachers and Coaches Can Stop the Violence, Harassment and Humiliation.* Hoboken, NJ: Jossey-Bass, 2006.

chapter 12

Camp, Jim. *Starting with No*. New York: Crown Business, 2002.

Fisher, Roger and William Ury. *Getting to Yes: Negotiating Agreement Without Giving In*. New York: Houghton Mifflin, 1992.

Masterson, Michael. *Power and Persuasion*. Hoboken, NJ: Wiley & Sons, 2005.

Index

About the Author

Ilise Benun is the founder of Marketing Mentor, as well as an author and national speaker. Her books include *Self-Promotion Online* and *Designing Web Sites:// for Every Audience* (HOW Design Books). She is also coauthor of *PR for Dummies, 2nd Edition.* She has been featured in national newspapers, including *The New York Times* and national magazines such as *Inc.* magazine, *Nation's Business, Self, Essence, Crains New York Business, HOW Magazine,* and *Working Woman.*

Benun publishes a free e-mail newsletter called *Quick Tips from Marketing Mentor,* that is read by more than 7,000 small business owners and has been excerpted in many other e-mail newsletters and on many Websites.

Benun has conducted workshops and given presentations for national and international trade organizations, including the American Marketing Association, the International Association of Business Communicators, the International Association of Business Leaders, the American Consultants League, the Business Marketing Association, the National Association of Women Business Owners,

219

the Family Business Council, the Downtown Women's Club, the American Writers and Artists Institute, the American Institute of Graphic Arts, the Graphic Artists Guild, NJ Creatives, the Registered Graphic Designers of Ontario, NY Designs—a program of LaGuardia Community College/CUNY, the NYU Entrepreneurship Summit, the Editorial Freelancers Association, WorldWIT (Women in Technology), the Usability Professionals Association, the HOW Design Conference, the NY Public Library, the 92nd St. Y, and ad clubs around the country.

Benun is also a board member of the Usability Professionals' Association (N.Y. Chapter) and Women in Cable and Telecommunications (N.Y. Chapter).

Benun's Marketing Mentor program is a one-on-one coaching program for small business owners who need someone to bounce marketing ideas off, and someone to be accountable to for their marketing. She started her Hoboken, N.J.-based consulting firm in 1988 and has been self-employed for all but three years of her working life. She has a B.A. in Spanish from Tufts University.

Ilise Benun can be reached at:
Marketing Mentor
P.O. Box 23
Hoboken, NJ 07030
Phone: 201-653-0783
Fax: 201-222-2494
E-mail: *ilise@marketing-mentor.com*
Website: *www.marketing-mentor.com*